25 Secrets to Sustainable Success

25 Secrets to Sustainable Success
A MASTER FIRM BUILDER BOOK

By Phillip C. Richards

GAMA International
Falls Church, Virginia

Leadership Unplugged is an imprint of GAMA International devoted to sharing the critical infrastructure of leadership practices that are fundamental to personal and professional success.

©2007 by GAMA International. All rights reserved.

Printed in the United States of America.

Except as permitted under the United States Copyright Act of 1976, no part of this publication may be reproduced or distributed in any form or by any means, or stored in a database or retrieval system, without prior written permission of the publisher.

Book design by Dee Bogetti

Acknowledgements

RIDING ATOP A miraculous rainbow for 45 years requires the help of many people. Trying to thank all of them would not only be impossible, it risks omitting some. But, just as in life, risk management is the business we are in, so let's give it our best shot.

It took a high school wrestling coach to plant the college seed in a boy whose family had never seen the eleventh grade. John Maitland, you altered my course for the better.

Maury Stewart was more than a perfect role model, he was a mentor, a leader and, after convincing me that this wonderful business was my destiny, became my friend. You changed my trajectory. I pray that I've passed your example on to others.

GAMA International has served as the "best practices" forum for all who have been wise enough to drink from that well. As my good friend, Luis Chiappy, said, "It is the one organization in the world that truly cares whether I have a job tomorrow." As another friend, Charlie Smith, publicly stated, "Cut my arm and you'll see GAMA blue flow." That says it all.

The love affair I've enjoyed for most of my career with Securian Financial has always been about people – about feelings, not figures. Integrity was the value woven through its fabric that served as the epoxy that fostered teamwork. Civility was the lubricant that made it work. Two chairmen, Coley Bloomfield and now Bob Senkler, have been the caretakers of a 125-year legacy of service in keeping long-term promises. Its many team members over the years, now led by Randy Wallake, continue the legacy and have validated the midwestern reputation for fairness and hard work.

To the other six members of "The Magnificent Seven" at Minnesota Mutual who essentially tendered their resignations to our board rather than serve the carpetbaggers attempting to hijack our company, Dick McCloskey, Bob Levitz, Nick Stevens, Larry Rybka, Dave Creamer and Norb Winter, you should all be in the hearts of policyholders who will never know your names or appreciate your willingness to sacrifice your contracts, if not your careers, for them. You are heroes.

Space prevents me from fully detailing the contributions of my fellow study group members, though many of the ideas in this book can be traced directly to strategies and tactics used in their firms. It's been said that stealing an idea from another is plagiarism, but stealing ideas from everyone is called research. The following study group members have provided much of the research herein: Al Granum, Maury Stewart, Charlie Smith, Jack Skalla, Gary Daniels, Gary Simpson, Joe Oakes, Mike O'Malley, Tim Flanagan, Tim Murray, Brud Hodgkins, Ron Lee, Bill Pollakov, Paul Blanco, Jeff Dollarhide, Steve Ford, Howard Elias, Linda Witham, Tim Schmidt, Chris Noonan, Norm Levine, Harry Hoopis, Bob Savage, Nick Horn, John Ackley, Ron Long, Dave Porter, John Langdon, John Baier, Luis Chiappy, Quincy Crawford, Wayne Swenson, Bob Baccigalupi, Howard Cowan, Ed Deutschlander, Greg Keller, Al Levitz, Paul Thomas and Jeff Golan.

I am grateful for all I have learned from the members of GAMA's Executive Management Cabinet, Conk Buckley, Lou DiCerbo, Mike White, Dick Miller, Dave Nelson, Mark Pfaff, Ron Rosbruch, Athan Vorilas, Burv Pugh, Jeff Hughes, Bill Cochran, Celeste Gurule, Bill Goodwin, Jim Mallon, John McTigue, Dick McCloskey and Burr Anderson, whose contributions form a good part of the bulwark of our shared world.

Along with the wisdom of all of the foregoing and sprinkled throughout this work are pass-ons from books that been have written by industry legends Norm Levine, Jim McCarthy, Bill Bachrach, Troy Korsgaden, Bob Krumroy, Bob Levitz, Norm Trainor, Lou Cassara, Jim Benson, Paul Karasik, Bill Wallace and Jack and Garry Kinder. If it's true that we are the sum product of everyone we've met and all that we've read, then surely I've been blessed with a bit of each and every one of you in me.

The world of many of us has expanded because of the contributions of giants outside of GAMA. The following leaders have faithfully carried the torch of "life" and deserve the gratitude of all of us: David Woods, Mike Vietri, Henry Hagan, John Greene, Fred Sievert, Chuck Wright, Dr. Larry Barton, Tom Burns, Dan Toran, Bill Beckley, Peter Browne, Jim Mitchell, Reggie Rabjohns, Steve Rothschild, Phil Harriman, John Prast, Bud Schiff, Jim Krueger, Art Kraus, Wayne Cotton and Czaba Sziklai.

I would be remiss if I failed to acknowledge my many friends in Thailand and especially Montri Saeng-Uraiporn who partnered with me and did most of the work in helping to create the thriving chapter of GAMA Thailand. You are the most gentle people on earth. Modh Amin in Singapore, Doctor Jack in Beijing, Cosmas Siblis in Greece, Michael Gau in Canada, Samuel Yung in Hong Kong and Peter Coyiuto in the Philippines have graced both GAMA and me with their commitment to face-to-face distribution and the miraculous product of life insurance.

As so many of you, I am compelled to recognize the many selfless contributions of the team members at GAMA International headquarters over these last 14 years that I have been involved with at the international level. MaryKay Myers, Jeff Hughes, Charlie Smith, Kathryn Kellam, Bonnie Godsman, et al. This organization serves its members well through the efforts of all of its volunteer practitioners, but the execution of those efforts is through and by all of you. On behalf of its more than 5000 members, I thank you.

Libbye Morris, Debra Grommons and Kathryn Kellam were selfless, patient and indispensable in the construction of this book and are responsible for the behind-the-scenes long hours in putting all of this together. Bob Kaufer and Loyall Wilson provided the compliance input that was essential and I am, of course, grateful to them as well. Without the five of them, this work would remain on the drawing board for a long time. If there are any errors herein, they are mine. Yet all of us endeavored to rush the work in time for

LAMP 2007 in keeping with the admonition, "a pretty good 'in-time' decision is infinitely better than a 'too-late' perfect one."

To my friends and associates at North Star who continue to do all of the work that I am so frequently credited with, I am forever indebted. Scott Richards, Dave Vasos, Ed Deutschlander, Diane Yohn, Shaun McDuffee and Don Schoeller serve as the bright light enabling others to see so clearly. You have grown so many that the future of our organization is a certainty. The advisors and team members who personify "Changing Lives, Forever®" and whose passion for our mission is boundless, provide the heart and soul of this work.

As you can see, there have been many to recognize because this has not been a one-man dog and pony show. Instead, any accomplishments that I have achieved in my career as well as my life have the "blended" imprint of each and every one of you.

And finally to my family, Christina, Kip, Scott, and my wife, Sue. Not only has your patience and understanding enabled me to devote a good part of my life to the profession that I so love, but your individual achievements have served as the major source of pride that has framed my career and been a wonderful source of inspiration. Thank you.

Wonder emanates from our own perspective. Wonder can be expressed when we stop taking things for granted. Wonder is contemplating the facts of life from a higher point of view. Wonder is remembering and acknowledging the uniqueness of our inner self. Of all the people in the world, there is only one of each of us. That is a wonder in itself. And it follows, then, that not only is each of us wonderful; each of us is a wonder. Situations and events are temporary. Wonder is perpetual. And so are you.

Gail Pursell Elliott

Phil Richards as an Easton High School senior in 1958.
Phil was a 3-year varsity wrestler.

Contents

Foreword by Maurice L. Stewart		xiii
Preface		xv
Introduction		xix
Chapter 1	Charting Your Course *Mission, Vision, and Values*	1
Chapter 2	Making Tough Decisions Easy	9
Chapter 3	Hire Slowly, Fire Quickly *Recycle People Into Different Roles*	17
Chapter 4	Cop, Coach, Community *From Autocracy to Interdependence*	33
Chapter 5	Chinese Table Tennis *Do What You're Best At; Delegate the Rest*	47
Chapter 6	Leading Through Teaching	57
Chapter 7	Servant Leadership *Great Leaders Are Servants First*	67
Chapter 8	The Mars Group *Creating the Infrastructure for Your Success*	79
Chapter 9	Focus on Relationships	91
Chapter 10	The Flywheel *Life Insurance Puts Client Relationships in Motion*	99
Chapter 11	People Love Specialists	107
Chapter 12	Blended, Not Balanced	117
Chapter 13	Goals Change Behavior	125
Chapter 14	Habits *All You Need Is 30 Days and a Commitment*	139
Chapter 15	20,000 Rejections	147
Chapter 16	Your Worst Deal Is Your Only Deal	153
Chapter 17	The Universal 80–20 Rule	159
Chapter 18	Create a Mentoring Culture *Increase Revenue, Decrease Costs*	165

Chapter 19	The Power of the Many *Study Groups for Managers and Advisors*	173
Chapter 20	Coach, Don't Coax	181
Chapter 21	A High-Performance, No-Excuse Culture	187
Chapter 22	Quarterly Reviews	195
Chapter 23	Expect Only What You Inspect	205
Chapter 24	Live Where You Want, With Those You Love, Doing the Right Work, on Purpose	211
Chapter 25	Think Tombstones *What Is Your Leadership Legacy?*	215
Epilogue		219
Appendix		233

Foreword

THERE ARE good people in the financial services industry, and there are some truly great people. The person I have the privilege of discussing here clearly ranks among the latter.

In 1962, when I met Phil Richards, I knew immediately that this young man possessed all the earmarks of a future leader, and he has certainly lived up to those expectations by becoming one of the industry's finest professionals.

Phil joined my agency in Philadelphia as a recent graduate of Temple University, eager to begin his career as a financial advisor. It wasn't long before he set the tone for our growing agency through his activity, productivity and integrity. In fact, the experienced associates in the agency, who seldom embraced new associates until they had proven themselves for several years, soon grew to admire and respect him.

This came as no surprise to me because his leadership ability had already manifested itself long before he joined my agency. As I researched his background, I found that Phil, extremely well respected by his professors, coach and fellow students, had been president of Temple's student body and captain of its wrestling team.

Many qualities distinguished Phil as a young producer. Most memorable among them were the tremendous energy level that he has maintained to this day, his outgoing personality and contagious enthusiasm. In addition, his integrity has always been beyond reproach.

Over time, Phil's leadership talent, as well as his production, placed him in a position to become a field leader. Unfortunately, at the time my company did not have an opportunity for Phil, so he chose to pursue his dream by leading a career agency with Minnesota Mutual. The rest, as they say, is history.

Over his 45-year career, Phil has built one of the largest and best agencies in the industry and the country. In addition to demonstrating his leadership in the field, Phil shared his expertise and talent with industry organizations – especially GAMA – where he served as president of GAMA International during one of the most critical years of its history. Under his leadership, GAMA prospered and thrived.

Phil's devotion to the Miracle of Life Insurance and the career-agency system has been demonstrated over and over again. His peers and the industry have honored him too many times to mention here, but when he was inducted into the GAMA International Management Hall of Fame, I was the proudest person in the room. In addition to his industry involvement, his civic activities are also numerous, including his stint as Chairman of the Better Business Bureau of the Twin Cities.

But all of Phil's great industry success pales in comparison to his devotion to his family and friends. His lovely wife, Sue, and their three children are the primary focus of his life – a trait you don't see that often in successful leaders.

Last but not least, Phil has never forgotten his friends and those who have been part of his growth. His loyalty to a wonderful guy who was in his recruiting class, Tom Vickers – and to his general agent, me, show the strength of his values and the commitment that he makes to his relationships. It is a privilege for me to say that Phil Richards is the finest leader I have ever known. I am honored to write this foreword and to consider him my friend.

Maurice L. Stewart, CLU ChFC CLF
Emeritus, Penn Mutual Insurance Company of America
GAMA International Management Hall of Fame (2004)

Preface

How the "25 Secrets" Came to Be

THE IDEA FOR this work began some 35,000 feet above the Pacific Ocean on a flight from Norita, Japan, to San Francisco. I was a past president of GAMA International, and GAMA's board of directors asked me to oversee its international committee, which involved an annual trip to Asia to present the GAMA value proposition and share the North Star story.

On most of these occasions, field leaders would approach the podium with the same request, and while it took many forms, it always amounted to, "Mr. Richards, I have listened intently to you for four (or six or eight) hours straight, and I have a question. What are the secrets, and what are the shortcuts?" My response was always the same: "There are no secrets, and there are no shortcuts."

Still, the refrain never ended. While the persistence of these leaders who wanted to grow was refreshing, it was also challenging. Sometimes they would say, "If you will just share the secrets with me, I won't tell anyone else." Still, as you know, there are no such things. Disappointing them unintentionally became part of an unwanted ritual.

As I mulled this conundrum after my flight took off, the thought snapped into my mind from thin air: "Why do I continue to disappoint these people whom I thoroughly like and enjoy? Why not just give them what they are asking for — the secrets and shortcuts? Even if I have to make them up!" With that, I took a yellow tablet from my case and wrote at the top of the page, "Phil Richards' 25 Secret Shortcuts to Agency Building." Within minutes, I crafted the best "drivers" I could think of that had accounted for North Star's success over the previous 35 years.

Once back in the office, I asked my executive assistant to type them onto a piece of paper in a space no bigger than a calling card. Next I asked her to get bids for the production of 5,000 of these cards, laminated, of course. The best bid she received was about $1,300, and she found out that it would take two weeks.

The following year, I arrived in Thailand and had dinner with my host, Montri Saeng-Uraiporn, the chief agency officer for GAMA Thailand, and gave him a box with 250 of the cards as a gift. Knowing that less than 30 percent of Thais read or write English and the audience was only going to be about 400 the following day, I thought that would be more than enough. The next morning, I arrived at the entrance to the meeting room at the hotel at 8:00 a.m. to see a huge crowd surrounding some tables. I approached the tables from the other side to see what the commotion was about, only to see cards very similar to my own being passed out to the attendees, and they were printed in Thai! I concluded that they were translated from my own because my name appeared at the top, in English.

Between 10:00 p.m. the previous evening and 8:00 a.m. that morning, Montri had translated the cards and had found a print shop that printed and laminated them, all for only $80. If I previously had any doubts as to just what formidable foes the emerging Asian nations would be, they were all dispelled that morning.

While I thought it was an amusing diversion at the time, compiling this list had an important outcome for me: it planted the seed that eventually became this book.

Here are the original "25 secret shortcuts":

Phil Richards' 25 Secret Shortcuts to Agency Building

1. Vision first, then strategy, tactics, execution
2. Client, customer, company — when values are clear, decisions are easy
3. Hire slow; fire fast; the 7/35 rule; energy + ethics; recycle
4. Cop, coach, consultant; dictatorship to interdependency
5. Chinese table tennis — do what you're best at; delegate the rest
6. Teach, teach, teach. Today's readers = tomorrow's leaders
7. Servant leadership; compliments are verbal sunshine; monthly notes reports

8. Think tombstones; growing others; changing lives forever
9. MARS Group — critical numbers; ownership; deadlines
10. Forget the computer — focus on creativity + relationships
11. Life insurance focus, the flywheel, controlling relationships, the miracle
12. Specialize — markets, recruits, products, services; people love specialists
13. Blended, not balanced, agents; praise publicly, criticize privately
14. Written goals — private- vs. public-domain BHAGs
15. Habits — 30-day rule; commitment, not involvement
16. 20,000 rejections — shorten the pain, videotape everything
17. Worst deal becomes your only deal — open book; fair, not equal
18. 80/20 rule applies to companies, agencies, agents
19. Mentoring culture increases revenue, decreases costs — GAMA/MDRT Mentoring
20. Study groups for managers; Sales Builder groups for agents
21. Coach, don't coax — who cares more; Coprolite
22. High-performance, no-excuse culture; freight train
23. Quarterly reviews; The Big Why; deliverables; no change — no change
24. Inspect what you expect; expect only what you inspect
25. Live where you want; with those you love; doing the right thing, on purpose

Be a Honeybee

While I don't believe that there are any secrets or shortcuts to success, it could be argued that learning best practices from our peers can be considered one. When we share our knowledge and wisdom, we are strengthening the industry so that more advisors can help more people experience the miracle of life insurance.

I started my career in this industry with one of the finest agency managers of all time, Maury Stewart, and I still use many of the effective strategies I learned from him. I've added to that arsenal by adopting and adapting many outstanding ideas from speakers at LAMP and MDRT, authors, businesspeople from around the world and other accomplished individuals. I would not be where I am today if it were not for others' willingness to share their best practices with me.

Now it's my turn to share my best practices, and this book is my way of giving back to a profession that has given me a quality of life that I never imagined possible and an opportunity to change other people's lives for the better.

Early on, I reasoned that my role was to be a honeybee – to take the nectar from one beautiful flower and pollinate the next. As field leaders, we are uniquely positioned to coach and lead advisors at the critical crossroads of their professional and personal lives. Doesn't it make sense for us to disseminate the powerful secrets of our success?

Some people have asked why I am not more hesitant to share my career secrets. First, I know that no one will use these strategies in exactly the same way that I do. It isn't just about the facts – it's the feeling, the instincts that make the difference. Reading this book gives people my tactics, but readers must follow their own instincts, must know the heartbeat of their own organizations' cultures and then must adapt the strategies to create their own success.

Most important, I do believe in the miracle of life insurance, and I want to do everything I can to help reach the millions of Americans who are uninsured or underinsured. If the lessons, successes and strategies North Star has experienced over four decades can help other field leaders and advisors insure more Americans, then this book has served its intended purpose.

Phillip C. Richards, CLU CFP RHU

Introduction

About North Star Resource Group

Building on the Vision of My Mentor

I HAD PLANNED to be a lawyer. In my senior year of college, I got married, and then I received a senatorial scholarship to Temple Law School at night. Our son was also born that year.

It was a tough year. I took a job that allowed me to work during the day and attend law school at night. But, two weeks after I got to law school, I realized that I hated it. I hated law, and I hated law school.

My day job was with Penn Mutual Life Insurance Company, drafting the Deposit Administration Group Annuity contract. One floor below me was the agency, which, at that time, was probably the largest in the world – Maury Stewart's agency. Maury recruited me into his agency at Penn Mutual.

I fell in love with Maury and the business. After my first year, I quit law school and went to work for Maury full-time. Maury used to say, "You're not in the life insurance business until the life insurance business is in you." When a manager buys into a vision – "Changing Lives, Forever®" for example, or "growing people" – and it gets inside the manager, then some big things begin to happen.

Maury always had a vision of growing people, of wanting people be the best they could be. The image Maury had in his mind of each of us who worked at Penn Mutual was bigger than the vision we had of ourselves.

I was with Maury at Penn Mutual from 1963 to 1965 and then joined Minnesota Mutual in 1966.

Professionalizing the Career

When I came into the industry, there was a perception in society that anyone could be an insurance agent. If you failed at other careers, you could always sell life insurance. That perception came about partly because of home collections – the debit man stopping at each client's house to pick up 17 cents every week. It was not considered a profession by any stretch of the imagination.

At North Star, we instituted four strategies to help professionalize the career: hiring college graduates, conducting all appointments in our office, broadening our product portfolio and serving a specialized clientele. The fourth strategy was one that Maury Stewart had embraced; he specialized in working with physicians. But the first three strategies came about after I became general agent of North Star in 1969.

Hiring College Graduates

We wanted to turn an industry that did not enjoy the best of reputations into a profession. So one year after I became the general agent of North Star, in 1970, I hired my first brand-new college graduate.

Hiring college graduates sent a message to people that not just anybody could sell insurance. To be hired at North Star, you had to have a college degree.

From that point on, we never turned back. Everybody who has come in here since has been a brand-new college graduate with no professional work history.

Conducting All Appointments in Our Office

In those days, insurance policies were sold at the client's kitchen table, usually after the breadwinner came home in the evening. To professionalize the career, we began requiring that all appointments take place in our office. Today, 99 percent of our appointments take place here. Physicians quit making house calls long ago, and we did the same.

Serving a Specialized Clientele

Another piece of our vision was to work only with professional, affluent people. We began with physicians. When we had too many advisors for the number of physician clients we had, we added dentists to our clientele. When we had too many advisors to serve physicians and dentists, we added veterinarians. Then we added pharmacists and engineers. Those were our five markets for three decades.

When we first started specializing, we did not allow advisors to do affinity marketing (to call on a friend, relative or neighbor) in their first year. We wanted them to make it on their own with the markets we gave them, either making cold calls on the telephone or calling on referred leads. Looking back, I see that that was a mistake because it limited our growth. It meant that the markets we were in dictated the number of people we could hire. If we had permitted people to use affinity marketing and call on their friends and relatives, who need those products just as much as physicians, dentists and engineers do, we would have been able to grow faster. It also would have enabled some people who did not make it in the business to succeed because they were natural affinity marketers but not good at cold-calling.

This approach did help professionalize the career, though. And there are people in our organization today who wouldn't have been here if we had been an affinity-marketing environment. They came here because it was a professional environment in which they could start working with other professionals immediately.

Today, we give our advisors a choice – they can come into our affinity-marketing program or our professional-marketing program.

Broadening Our Product Portfolio

Remember, we had only fixed products in those days – no variable products were available. But some of our clients were indicating that they wanted to expose their money to growth risk and invest in the stock market. So we began selling mutual funds. I was licensed in

1969 to sell securities, and we required every one of our advisors to get their securities licenses along with their life and health licenses.

That gave our advisors a competitive advantage. Whether it was sustainable or not, we didn't know. It was new. Our only competitor in Minneapolis was Clair Strommen, who ran the organization that was the predecessor to Swenson Anderson Associates. Clair went on to be president and CEO of what is now Thrivent Financial for Lutherans. He was the only other person selling mutual funds.

Selling mutual funds was such a departure from the norm 35 years ago that it actually got me kicked out of a local GAMA chapter.

The world 35 years ago was quite different, and those in the life insurance business understandably dealt in black and white terms, meaning certainties and not chance. The use of a chance commodity like stocks was anathema to the majority at the time. In 1971, Lynn Nord of MassMutual invited me to join the Board of the Minneapolis General Agents and Managers Association. I had been a general agent in the city for about two years at the time. Two years later, I received a call from another board member asking me to resign from the board because of differing philosophies among us – the fact that North Star at the time billed itself as a financial planning firm and was selling mutual funds to its clients.

There were no hard feelings on either side, and everyone concluded that honest men can differ on certain things.

How things change! Thirty years later, I was honored to serve GAMA International as its president. At North Star, we continued to do things precisely the same as we had always done them, but the industry made a 180-degree turn, from risk-based advice to total financial planning. The irony increased in intensity when, in 1998, GAMA President Dick McCloskey asked me to chair GAMA's financial partners' program to raise money for GAMA from mutual fund companies. I did so, and we raised more than $1 million dollars in just two years.

North Star Today

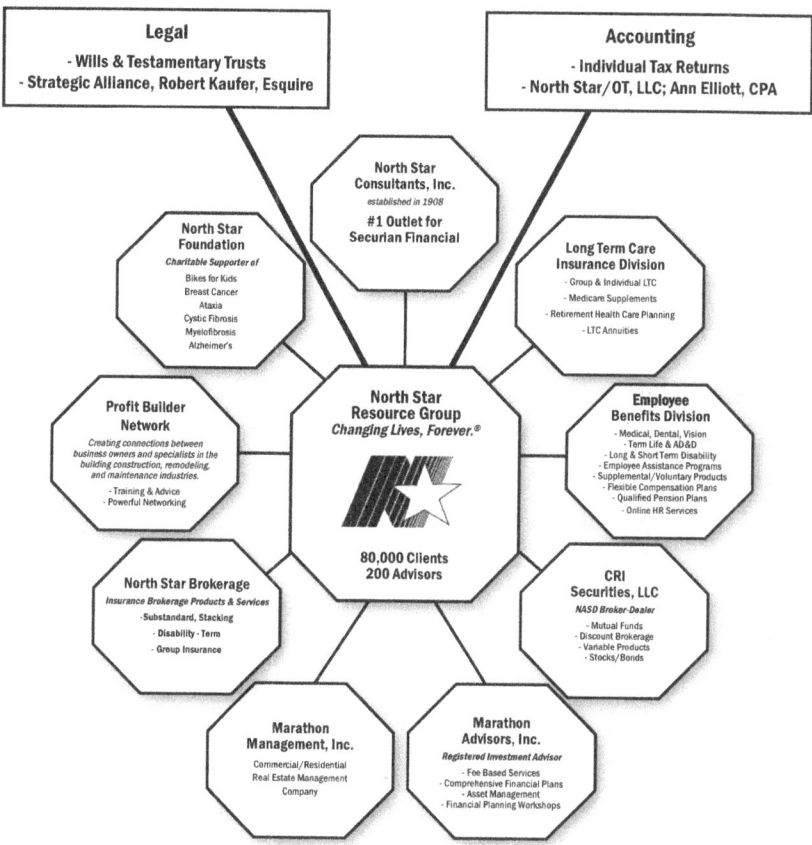

What is known today as the North Star Resource Group can trace its genesis to the Eliason Agency, which was formed in 1908 in Minnesota and is proud to have an unbroken record of service to its clients to this day.

North Star serves a specialized clientele composed of physicians, dentists, veterinarians, engineers and small-business owners. To serve these professional markets, North Star recruits advisors exclusively from college campuses, hiring only college graduates most of whom have finished in the top quarter of their class.

Today we have nine separate but interrelated entities providing a broad range of services. Our legal and accounting divisions serve all of them. To show how they work together, we created the above "pinwheel." Clients and advisors are in the center – clients because, of course, we couldn't be in business without them (and shouldn't be, either) and advisors because they control the client relationships. They're the axle that turns the wheel; they are the driving force of North Star's very existence.

The North Star Charitable Foundation

It may seem odd to include the North Star Charitable Foundation on the wheel, but we wanted to expand our "Changing Lives, Forever"® mission into the community. We established the North Star Financial Charitable Foundation in 2003. The foundation is dedicated to contributing the greater of $100,000 or 10 percent of profits to worthwhile charitable causes. Currently, the foundation supports Alzheimer's, ataxia, breast cancer, cystic fibrosis and Myelofibrosis charities.

A sixth endeavor, Bikes for Kids, provides bicycles to hundreds of underprivileged children in the Minneapolis/Saint Paul area.

Led by North Star's Executive Vice President Ed Deutschlander, his wife Toni and many North Star team members, the Bikes for Kids event provided 353 new bikes to children in December 2006 at an exciting event that the children attended with their parents at the Metrodome. The Minnesota Twins team helped make the event memorable by providing dinner, letting the children play on the professional sports field and spending time with them.

I know that the children who receive these bicycles will remember the gift for a lifetime. I used to be one of those kids and I remember numerous events that The Boys Club of New York sponsored when I was a child. Just when I thought no one gave a darn, another event happened. I appeared on the Howdy Doody television show five years in a row, saw the Ringling Brothers Barnum & Bailey Circus five times at Madison Square Garden, visited the Bronx Zoo frequently, attended two or three Major League Baseball games each year and met and shook hands with Joe DiMaggio. I also met Yogi Berra, Roy Rogers, Gene Autry and William Boyd (Hop Along Cassidy)

These opportunities left an indelible mark on me, and it's important to me that our firm gives back to the community so that disadvantaged children can have happy memories that will last them a lifetime. Believe me, they don't ever forget. The North Star Charitable Foundation allows us to change children's lives, forever.

Sailing Toward Further Success

I chose a nautical theme for this book because I love the water. When I was a child, my dream was to attend the U.S. Naval Academy in Annapolis, Maryland. I wanted to be a sailor.

When I had enough money to go to the movies at the Bijou Theater on Avenue B in New York City at the end of World War II, I was fascinated by the stark contrast on the big screen between the dashing Navy officers in their clean, white uniforms and the frantic soldiers scrambling around in foxholes in dirty uniforms. I wanted to be a Navy officer in a pristine white uniform.

As I grew up, I became aware of another reason to attend the U.S. Naval Academy: my single mother could not afford to send me to college, and a Navy career could provide me with a free education. As I explain in Chapter 13, unique circumstances caused me to miss the chance to achieve my dream of a career in the Navy, but the new path my life took led me to the insurance and financial services industry.

The nautical theme is also a fitting metaphor for how we manage North Star Resource Group toward further success. Our values guide us through storms and calms alike. They don't change.

With this book, I invite you to share in our stories, to experiment with our techniques and to take the helm yourself to use our hard-won knowledge to guide your own organizations to far-reaching and sustainable success.

Chapter 1

Charting Your Course
Mission, Vision and Values

IN THE CLASSIC book *The Little Prince*, the fox states to the prince, "Anything essential is invisible to the eyes."[1] Your mission, vision and values statements form the invisible but absolutely essential foundation for your success. They are the core by which everything else you do is measured.

When I acquired the insurance component of North Star in 1969, we had five advisors and employees. Today we have 350 team members in all of the affiliated companies that operate under North Star Resource Group. To ensure that we have synergy throughout the organization, we must hire the right people into the right positions, and we must operate in ways that keep all functions and processes aligned. To accomplish this, we share a common vision of where we are headed, a common set of values by which we all abide, and a common mission that fills us with purpose.

---

[1] Antoine de Saint-Exupéry and Richard Howard (translator), *The Little Prince*, Harcourt, Inc., Orlando, Fla., 1943 and 1971, p. 63.

Mission

Your *mission* is your purpose — the reason your business exists. A true mission is bigger than simply "making a profit" or "selling insurance." It is the larger purpose behind those activities that gives meaning to your professional and personal life.

At North Star, our mission is "Changing Lives, Forever®." If you ask the receptionist at North Star what we do, she'll say, "We change lives." We change the lives of our advisors, who, in turn, change the lives of our clients and their families. Because of our products and our advisors' good planning, businesses keep running and people stay employed when owners die, and families are permitted to remain in their homes, schools, churches and communities when breadwinners perish. And they do perish, each and every day.

Southwest Airlines is a great example of a company that has achieved success while pursuing a noble mission — to let poor people fly the same as rich people. By 2005, Southwest Airlines had been profitable every year for 31 years and ranked high in employee satisfaction and retention.[2] Profitability isn't their mission, but they have achieved it through the effective execution of a noble purpose, which is to democratize flying.

It has been said that people work for one of five reasons: money, fame, power, a leader or a cause. Of those, cause is the one most in our control. Create this cause — your mission — and people will beat a path to your door.

Vision

Your *vision* is what you want your organization to become. It describes what the future looks like. Jack Welch, former CEO of GE, said, "Good business leaders create a vision, passionately own the vision and relentlessly drive it to completion."

---

[2] Jody Hoffer Gittell, *The Southwest Airlines Way*, The McGraw-Hill Companies, New York, 2005, p. 3.

Our vision at North Star was "to be the best and biggest client-centered, independent financial resource firm in the world." In 2005, we achieved that lofty dream.[3]

As a result, in 2006 our organization developed a new vision to replace the one that was no longer relevant. Our new vision is "to be an unwavering client advocate committed to building irreplaceable relationships for life." It is important to note the all-inclusive nature of two words — "client" includes both advisors and their clientele, and "life" covers both the full measure of one's time on Earth as well as our miraculous product, life insurance.

My earliest brush with what vision can do and how it can energize people was when my colleague, Ed Deutschlander, shared this quote by Johann Goethe:

> "If I accept you as you are, I will make you worse.
> However, if I treat you as though you are
> what you are capable of becoming,
> I help you become that."

That's a vision that each of us can have about everybody whose lives we touch on a daily basis. If I treat you as the person you think you are instead of as the person I know you can become, I'm not helping you. Your vision of yourself and your abilities remains the same and may even diminish. But if I treat you as if you are better than you think you are, then you begin to believe *my* elevated vision of you and live up to it. It works that way because that's the way most of us are hardwired.

In 1966, I was fortunate enough to lead Hartford Life in sales using a simple concept with HR-10 plans (similar to today's simplified employee plans). Discovering that the income tax brackets of single, widowed or divorced individuals were approximately 50 percent higher than those of married people, I prospected only in that segment of the small-business market because of the competitive

---

[3] In 2005, GAMA International ranked North Star No. 2 in the world behind the largest organization, which was a wholly owned branch office and not considered independent.

advantage gained from the extra leverage of additional tax savings. When asking for referred leads, I used the customary question: "Whom do you know who is successful and in business for himself or herself?" But I also asked, "Who is single, widowed or divorced?" I sold 43 retirement plans that year for very large premiums with a simple concept.

As you know, no good deed goes unpunished. In January 1967, my manager called me in to tell me that I was not allowed to sell anymore HR-10 plans because I was "in a rut and not growing." From that point forward, I would be confined to corporate pensions only.

As you might imagine, I was more than a bit disappointed. But the point I learned was that his dream for me and the total professional he wanted me to become was bigger than mine. He was not tempted by the easy money that was coming in as a result of my streak, but instead was committed to a more experienced and more versatile Phil in the future. I realized that I had hit the jackpot — I had a leader who wanted to grow others.

I often refer to Jim Collins' book, *Good to Great*. The single issue I take with that work is his contention that you should first get good people on the bus, and then you can figure out where to drive it.[4] Through my experience, and intuitively, I believe that just the opposite is true — your vision must come first. The best way to get good people on your bus is to have a vision that inspires them. I don't believe that the best people will get on a bus if they don't know where it's going.

Imagination is essential. "The ability to see, to imagine how things can be" is how Curt Carlson, who built Carlson Companies, one of the largest private companies in the world, described his success. He said, "I'm not distracted by how things are." Carlson started his company in 1938 with an idea and a $55 loan. When he died in 1999, Carlson Companies was doing business in more than 140

---

[4] Jim Collins, *Good to Great: Why Some Companies Make the Leap... And Others Don't*, HarperCollins Publishing Inc., New York, 2001, p. 13.

countries and employing nearly 150,000 people, and *Forbes* magazine estimated Carlson's net worth at $1.6 billion.[5]

Values

Values define expected behaviors in your organization — how you will interact with each other and with your clients. They are the principles and beliefs that guide you in your daily operations. Values are constant. While your mission and vision may evolve over time, they will be shaped by the core values that you have subscribed to for most of your life.

One of North Star's values is to do the right thing when no one is looking — otherwise known as integrity. Integrity is the "I" in the acronym FIGS, which, as we discuss in Chapter 2, represents North Star's core values: faith, integrity, growth and service.

The book *Built to Last* looks at the differences between extraordinary ("visionary") companies and merely good ("comparison") companies.[6] For example, the authors said that the difference between the visionary (and industry-leading) Merck and the comparison pharmaceutical company, Pfizer, was that Merck's values were focused on helping people while Pfizer was more focused on making a profit. Around the same time that Merck's president stated, "Medicine is for the patient ... the profits follow," Pfizer's president said, "So far as is humanly possible, we aim to get profit out of everything we do."[7]

Merck's values aren't just nice sentiments put on paper. They have stood by those values. After World War II, Japan was suffering from widespread tuberculosis. When the Japanese government couldn't afford to pay for streptomycin, Merck gave it to them. Why? Because the company wanted to preserve and improve human life.[8]

---

[5]Mark Zdechlik, "Curt Carlson Obit," Minnesota Public Radio, February 22, 1999, downloaded from www.mpr.org on December 27, 2006.
[6]Jim Collins and Jerry I. Porras, *Built to Last: Successful Habits of Visionary Companies,* HarperCollins Publishers Inc., New York, 1994 and 1997.
[7]Collins, *Good to Great,* p. 49.
[8]Collins and Porras, *Built to Last,* p. 47.

Is it any wonder that today, Merck is the largest non-Japanese pharmaceutical company in Japan?

Examples of Successful Organizations' Purpose and Inspiration

The business world is replete with examples of organizations that have a compelling purpose and noble values. People can't wait to jump on those buses because they want to be a part of a compelling journey.

One of my favorite examples of an organization with a noble purpose is the Mayo Clinic, which abides by the principle that the best interest of the patient is the only interest to be considered.[9]

Here are additional examples:[10]

3M: To solve unsolved problems innovatively.

Cargill: To improve the standard of living around the world.

Mary Kay Cosmetics: To give unlimited opportunity to women.

Merck: To preserve and improve human life.

Nike: To experience the emotion of competition, winning and crushing competitors.

Wal-Mart: To give ordinary folk the chance to buy the same things as rich people.

Walt Disney: To make people happy.

Execution of Strategies and Tactics

Formulating and communicating your mission, vision and values, while vital, is only the beginning. You must ensure that your business policies and processes are aligned with these driving factors and contribute to them. And then you must create and execute the strategies required to achieve them. (We talk more about execution in Chapter 23.)

---

[9] Richard Normann and Niklas Arvidsson, eds., *People as Care Catalysts: From Being Patient to Becoming Healthy*, John Wiley & Sons Ltd., Chichester, United Kingdom, 2006, p. 122.
[10] Collins and Porras, *Built to Last*, p. 225.

During more than 40 years in this rewarding industry, we have had many successes and, naturally, made many mistakes at North Star. We have used those learning experiences to help refine the strategies that drive us toward our own mission and vision. In this book, I share those experiences with you, my fellow field leaders, so that you can learn from our mistakes and adapt our successes to your own environment and culture.

The strategies presented in this book are the tangible, manageable elements that will help you and your team bring your mission, vision and values statements alive with activity, energy and passion.

> *Your vision will become clear only when you look into your heart. Who looks outside, dreams.*
> *Who looks inside, awakens.*
>
> CARL JUNG

You Take the Helm

- **Find Your Mission** — What is the noble cause that fills you with purpose? Purpose is powerful. It energizes people far more than profits do. The profits will follow.

- **Create Your Vision** — Think huge. Imagination, not reality, is the bedrock of your vision. See people and things as they can be, not as they are. When asked if there was anything worse than blindness, Helen Keller replied, "To be without vision."

- **Define Your Values** — Identify and communicate the core principles and beliefs that will guide you and your team in everything you do.

- **Execute** — Build the organization you deserve to have.

Chapter 2

Making Tough Decisions Easy

AS A COLLEGE freshman, I read a biography of a philosopher named Benedict de Spinoza (1632–77), a lens grinder whose birth name was Baruch Spinoza. He was born, lived in and died in the Netherlands. His Portuguese Jewish family had fled to the Netherlands as refugees from the Spanish Inquisition.[1] While alive, he was referred to as an atheist, but after his death he became known as "a God-intoxicated man." Spinoza was a leading philosophical thinker, considered by subsequent philosophers to be one of the three major Rationalist philosophers of his time.

Spinoza is well known for his argument against the existence of free will. He refers to a metaphor of a jackass standing at the juncture of a road. The ass is equally thirsty and hungry and must decide between walking down one path to food and walking down another path to water. But because the food and water are equally far away, the ass is immobilized by indecision and subsequently dies of both hunger and thirst.[2] While other philosophers argued that surely a

---

[1] R. Scruton, *Spinoza: The Great Philosophers Series,* Routledge, New York, 1999, p. 3.
[2] Michael Losonsky, *Enlightenment and Action from Descartes to Kant: Passionate Thought*, Press Syndicate of the University of Cambridge, United Kingdom, 2001, p. 150.

human wouldn't starve because a human would freely choose one or the other, Spinoza argued there is no such thing as free choice, and so the human would indeed starve, just like the jackass.[3]

In leadership roles, we are often called upon to make difficult decisions. This conundrum is no different from the one that the donkey faced. As the story illustrates, there is a line of reasoning that tells us that if the call is that close, then the way that we choose our priorities won't really matter.

I don't subscribe to that line of reasoning. I believe that humans do have a free will to make choices. And I believe that we make our best choices when we consciously use our values to guide our decision-making process.

Values Affect Decisions

Roy Disney, one of the architects of the Disney family's world-renowned management success, said, "When values are clear, decisions are easy."[4] This is probably the most often-repeated phrase at North Star, and for good reason.

We are the end product of all the experiences we have lived through, all of the people with whom we have come into contact, and all of the things we have ever read. These are the things that shape who we are. They form the values that, in turn, make our decisions easy — if we allow them to.

Here is a technique that we at North Star have found valuable. The next time you are faced with an important decision, write down your most compelling values, those things you believe in and live by. Then write down the problem. You'll find that the decision will emerge automatically. It's a great exercise. It has always amazed me that a decision that seems so difficult at first suddenly becomes so easy.

---

[3]Georgetown University, "Last Lecture on Spinoza's Theory of Mind," http://www.georgetown.edu/faculty/ap85/471/LastLectureOnSpinozasTheoryOfMind.html, downloaded October 19, 2006.
[4]Bill Capodagli and Lynn Jackson, *The Disney Way Fieldbook: How to Implement Walt Disney's Vision of Dream, Believe, Dare, Do in Your Own Company,* McGraw-Hill, New York, 2000, p. 122.

We had a Court of the Table advisor in one of our branch offices who didn't share most of our values. For years, he interviewed with our competitors for better compensation. Finally, we learned that he had almost committed to go with a competitor and was simultaneously undermining our relationships with other advisors in that office. Firing a Court of the Table producer was not a welcome event, especially when he didn't want to be terminated. We debated about what we should do.

But all we had to do was look at our clear values and ask ourselves, "Do we believe in empowering our regional vice presidents (RVPs)?" Yes. Then it should be the RVP's call. "Do we value honesty and transparency?" Absolutely! "Do we believe in putting our clients' welfare first?" Of course. And in response to this last question, our RVP asked out loud, "If this advisor was dishonest about his intentions with us, can he be trusted to do the right thing with our clients when no one is looking?" We realized that we might have an integrity issue on our hands. Our RVP independently made the call and terminated the advisor the very next day, effective immediately. No one in our organization looked back. It was the right thing to do. What an easy decision to make once we reviewed our values!

When your values are clear, your decisions are easy. Unless you are trying to learn from a decision and improve yourself, never look back. When others are looking around, leaders look straight ahead. Farmers say that you can't plow a furrow by looking back; leaders can't lead except by focusing on their straight-ahead vision.

At North Star, the shared values that help us look straight ahead at North Star form the acronym FIGS: Faith, Integrity, Growth and Service.

Faith
Including faith as a corporate value was something of a challenge for us. On one hand, most, if not all, of our team members and advisors strongly believe in a supreme being and would agree that faith is not everything, but it does rank up there with food and oxygen. Others believe that expressions of these convictions should

be off-limits in the workplace and our firm. Our Corporate Development Council (which we formed by completing the "Mars Group" exercise described in Chapter 8) decided that faith is a generous word with multiple meanings. To a person in the latter camp, it can mean faith in one another, in our organization, in the correctness of our cause, in our leadership, in the confidence in our back-office experts or in our partner, Securian.

Regardless of how you define it, faith is an important value. Erich Fromm said, "Only a person who has faith in himself is able to be faithful to others." Cicero said, "A man of courage is also full of faith."

Integrity

Integrity speaks for itself. We are in two businesses simultaneously: a people business and a money business. We are the hope of many for their risk management, asset accumulation, retirement and estate liquidation. Anything less than complete integrity is unacceptable. Hiring young people right out of college is in harmony with this value. At the very time in their careers when they are forming their vocational value systems, we hire them into a culture that cherishes integrity and executes a "client comes first" priority system.

Growth

Growth means many things to us. First is our belief in lifelong learning. Unless a person is committed to this proposition, a life of relentless atrophy is predictable. Choosing a life of continuous improvement rather than presiding over a decaying mind seems like a given. Unfortunately, not everyone agrees. Growth is not an accident but rather the progressive realization of a conscious purpose, followed by determined execution. Look at the leaders of any organization, and the validity of this concept becomes evident. Robert Schuller said, "Unless I am expandable, I am expendable."

Growth also means striving to be better at our vocation. We are all given talents and abilities, and our mission should be to use them effectively. The United Negro College Fund had it right when it coined the phrase, "A mind is a terrible thing to waste."

Service

Service is our fourth value. At the management level, we are committed to servant leadership, a concept we discuss in Chapter 7. Our advisors are *our* customers; their clients are *their* customers. We should serve the advisors just as they serve their clients. Ten years ago, customers would stay with you unless you did something that caused them to leave. Today, they'll leave you unless you give them a reason to stay.

Our commitment to servant leadership and our values paves the way for our decisions. Service to one's fellow man is the rallying cry. Having a positive impact on people is the noble calling. Serving others is the worthy cause.

Mentorship, an important part of our organization's culture, supports this concept because it involves giving back to the industry by helping others. That generosity is the very value that catapults great men and women to the top. At the end of the day, it's only those things we've given away that we take with us.

It has been said that prayers may or may not change things, but they do change the people who say them. Even without considering the impact that we have on others, serving them will change *us* for the better.

Priorities: Client, Customer, Company

Because of our commitment to serving others, we place the needs of our policyholders at the top of our priority list. Our second priority is our advisors. The organizations that manufacture and distribute the products — our company and our firm, respectively — are third. It is not that companies are unimportant. They are vital. However, today's issues do not involve a shortage of manufactured products, but rather insufficient distribution. More than 30 years ago, Peter Drucker said that manufacturing was king in 1970, distribution would be king in 2000 and the consumer would be king in 2030.

Having our priorities in order — client, customer, company — makes it easy for us to make decisions on a daily basis.

These priorities should be self-evident. Our clients must come first, and our advisors must come next. If that is not the case, then let's close up shop and all go home. Our dedication to our clients and advisors is what separates us from the transaction jockeys in our industry, and it characterizes our way of life as relationship driven rather than focused on commodities.

We hired a great advisor a few years ago who clearly understood that the client must come first. He had interned with a major securities wirehouse for three months but eventually decided to come to work with us. When he was asked why he chose North Star over the much better offer he got from that much better-known company, he explained that during his internship there, all he experienced were high-fives when big sales were made, and the best interests of the client were rarely a reason for the celebration. He *got* it!

Clients Are More Loyal to Advisors Than to Companies

Most managers would probably agree that the consumer should be the first priority. Yet some people in this industry do not agree that our advisors — our customers — should be the second priority. They contend that the company should come second.

But this is not a question of what someone thinks *should* happen. It's a matter of how the sales process actually works, and anyone who has ever sold our products knows the process. Let me explain.

A few years ago, I was asked to address a conference of about 300 home-office employees in Toronto. In my presentation, I stated that policyholders are customers of the advisor, not of the home office. The reaction of that audience was one of absolute incredulity.

As proof of this position, I explained to the audience that when an advisor leaves one company to migrate to another, as happens all too frequently, clients follow the advisor rather than stay with the company. When that advisor leaves, persistency plummets, costing the company huge dollars. The client rarely buys more insurance or securities from that company, but instead follows the advisor to his or her new company. So the pertinent question becomes, who influences the behavior of the clients? The advisor does so much more than the company. We're in a people business where relationships and trust rule the day.

Later I asked the audience, "After the sale is made, what is invariably the next question that the prospect or client will ask?" You could have heard a pin drop in that meeting. There was no answer, evidence of how few of them had ever sold our product. So I explained that the question that clients ask immediately after a sale is, "Who should I make the check out to?" Anyone who has ever sold a life insurance product knows that the client will write the check out to whomever the advisor says. One needs no further proof that the advisor is the one who controls the sale — not the policyholder, not the manager, and certainly not the firm or the company.

A quality advisor helps clients recognize and clarify their personal values, leading them to purchasing decisions they can feel good about. Clients' loyalties belong to their advisors — our customers.

> *When values are clear, decisions are easy.*
> Roy Disney

You Take the Helm

- **Define Your Values** — Faith, integrity, growth and service (FIGS) are our values. What are yours?

- **Use Your Values to Make Decisions** — When faced with a difficult decision, write down your values and then write down the problem you are struggling with. Your decision will emerge automatically.

- **Set Your Priorities** — Once you have your priorities in order and in tune with your values, your decisions become easy.

- **Don't Delay a Decision** — A good "in time" decision is always better than a perfect "too late" decision.

- **Don't Look Back After a Decision** — Do the best that you can, and then move on. Remember what Shakespeare said in *Macbeth*: "Things without all remedy should be without regard. What's done is done."

- **Treat Your Advisors Like Customers** — Clients are loyal to the advisors they know and trust. This underscores the high value that you should place on your advisors, who are in fact *your* customers.

Chapter 3

Hire Slowly, Fire Quickly

Recycle People Into Different Roles

AS A PERSON of Sicilian descent who has been to the island of Sicily more than a dozen times to tour and to visit relatives, I have been fascinated over the years by the island's history — including the history of the Sicilian Mafia. Much research has been done on the topic, but I will share only the information I have garnered firsthand, since I am not sure of the accuracy of many of the commonly circulated stories.

My understanding is that the word "mafia" is derived from Arabic and means "a place of refuge, a sanctuary." In the last 2,000 years, Sicily, strategically located in the center of the then-known Western world, has been invaded and inhabited by more than 20 foreign conquerors. The people of the island felt the need to create their own protection against foreign oppression — a government within the realm of the governance of their conquerors. That inside entity became known as the Mafia, and it started out with noble aims, serving as an instrument for justice and protection. Unfortunately, like many entities before and since, it became corrupt, with Machiavellian means and self-serving ends. It turned to violence and worse in the ensuing decades.

I heard about this history directly from people who I knew had lived in western Sicily in the 19th century, and the concept fascinated me. The organization may have been corrupt, but good and God-fearing people loved and respected it. Incredible and illogical!

While thinking about what a firm in our industry should look like, the term "sanctuary" kept recurring in my mind. A sanctuary is what advisors should expect, especially in the beginning of their careers when they are overworked, underpaid and subject to constant rejection.

It is our function as managers to create a supportive, caring environment to help our advisors deal with those initial overwhelming challenges. When we build an agency or firm, what we're really doing is much like creating an extended family. We're creating a support system where people reinforce one another — especially new advisors — in this very difficult and challenging environment. We strive to construct a familial environment, a home away from home. And as leaders, we must be vigilant in protecting the integrity of this sanctuary to keep it from being corrupted by incompatible values, or atrophying from neglect.

Each time we hire a new person into this familial atmosphere, it changes the dynamics of the organization. Just as the moon's gravitational pull on the Earth causes a shift in ocean currents and levels, it affects all of us to varying degrees.

Each new person will affect your organization either positively or negatively. So hire slowly. You want to make sure that, to the best of your ability and within the confines of the systems that you're using to identify good people, you choose those candidates whose pull on your organization will be in the right direction.

About 30 years ago, I interviewed a candidate who was eventually turned down. He was hired by another firm, went on to become a perennial Million Dollar Round Table (MDRT) and Top of the Table performer, and has on at least two occasions been a main-platform presenter at MDRT. When I have attended industry meetings where he has been the featured speaker, he has jokingly pointed me out in the audience as the general agent who turned him down. I don't take it personally because I know that it was not for lack of promise that he was not hired, but rather for my opinion that he did not have a cultural fit with our firm. I'm sure to this very day that neither of us regrets the decision I made, and we remain friends.

The Significance of Age Seven

During the time of the Spanish Inquisition, the Catholic clergy in Spain educated and ordained as priests orphan boys who were brought from foreign lands that Spain had conquered. These youngsters were transported to Spain and placed in a highly regimented but very nurturing environment to become future Jesuit priests. The boys were leaving one life of poverty for another, but one with respect and privilege.

The Jesuits passed on an important saying: "Give me the boy until he's seven, and I'll give you back the man, and you won't change him much." I subscribe to this belief, and it is very important to me, realizing that in my own case, many of my early experiences have molded me into the person I have become. It's the reason I'm so in favor of programs like Head Start that support disadvantaged children as early in life as possible. These children will be fed properly; begin believing in themselves; develop a positive self-image; and receive leadership, teaching and education at an early age — the earlier the better. Our prisons are full of many people who didn't have those advantages and who might very well not be there if they had.

A recent *Business Week* article provides quantitative proof that providing aggressive preschool education for children from troubled homes yields extraordinary dividends for the families and society. Waiting until elementary school or later to give these children extra attention doesn't pay off.[1]

---

[1] Christopher Farrell, "Programs that Put Real Money into Intensive Preschooling Pay Off — In Productive Workers," *Business Week,* October 23, 2006, p. 108.

The article points to a 40-year study of 123 children in Michigan. From 1962 through 1967, preschool teachers worked intensively with 64 low-income African-American children aged 3 to 4, both at preschool and once a week in their homes. Forty years later, administrators compared the children's life stories with those of 59 who did not receive special attention. The payoff was impressive. Almost half of the preschooled children performed at grade level by the age of 14, compared with just 15 percent in the control group, and 60 percent were earning at least $20,000 a year in their 40s, versus 40 percent in the control group. Throw in the higher number of school grades completed, the lower rates of criminal activity, less time spent in prison and other factors, and the benefit-to-cost ratio comes to $17 for every $1 invested. "The research is overwhelming," says Arthur J. Rolnick, director of research at the Federal Reserve Bank of Minneapolis and an enthusiastic supporter of such programs. "It all comes down to 'the earlier, the better.'"[2]

Incidentally, Dr. Rolnick is the father of one of North Star's very successful advisors, Andrew Rolnick.

The 7/35 Rule

The evidence is overwhelming that most of our true character is formed by the time we are seven years old, and we do not change very much after that. So in North Star's interviewing process, we constantly try to find out about our candidates' early childhood memories.

The "7/35 rule" is a quick way of referring to the idea that people develop their core personality features by age seven, and they have generally progressed as far as they might in life by age 35. Once people turn 35, they have little chance of changing significantly. At that point, they have, for the most part, become the people they will be. This constancy is the reason that psychological tests can provide us with valuable insights.

So in the interview process, we dig deeply to find out just who and what that seven-year-old child was like. A key question we ask

[2]Farrell, pp. 108 and 110.

is, "Tell me the earliest thing you remember. How far back can you go?" What you are trying to determine is attitude. We've learned that positive people will think of a positive experience, like "I got a beautiful red bike for Christmas. That is the first thing I remember. I couldn't have been three years old, but I remember that beautiful red bike." A negative person tends to remember a negative experience, such as, "I fell off my red bike and tore a hole in my knee. I had to go to the hospital for stitches, and I remember crying the whole time."

I believe that roughly the same number of positive and negative things happen to most of us. But positive people will go back and dwell on good experiences. They focus on good memories. Those are the people we want working with us. So we want to find out what and who the positive people were by the time they were seven years old.

A second question we ask is, "In what ways do you think you're the same and in what ways do you think you're different from the child you were at age seven? How do you think you've changed?" Now, remember what our premise is — we don't think they *have* changed, or if they have changed, then not very much. That's what my psychologist friends tell me — people change, but not much.

Does that mean that people cannot change? No. People can change dramatically, but not in ways that we laymen can control. One way is to have brain surgery. That could certainly affect someone's personality or view of life. Another way is to have a complete religious conversion of some kind — throwing yourself on your knees and into the hands of an almighty God. That could work. A third thing that might work is years of therapy. But these are not common, everyday occurrences, and we certainly can't implement them.

It doesn't matter what interviewees say in response to the question about how they think they've changed. We want to know what they thought their attitude was when they were seven years old and what they think it is today. They are, for the most part, the same person they were at seven. They've had other influences and they may have marginally changed, but, as an example, if their early experiences caused them to hate people, then there's a good chance that they won't have a great attitude toward other people as an adult.

Psychologists Agree

This idea really started to gel for me when we used a psychologist to screen all of our serious prospects. In fact, it was such an effective selection tool that Minnesota Mutual began using this process nationally.

The psychologist conducted a battery of tests that took almost three hours, including a 45-minute interview with each candidate. We received a written psychological evaluation for each person, along with a recommendation to either hire or decline. At the time, it cost us $500 for each candidate.

The psychologist was instrumental in keeping our retention rate high because we greatly reduced our hiring mistakes.

After a decade or so, we stopped using the program. We had become good enough at learning what the psychologist looked for that we brought the process in-house. Minnesota Mutual did the same thing at about the same time, but for different reasons.

During all those years of seeing hundreds of psychological evaluations, I observed what the Jesuits talked about — that people, to a great extent, become who they are by the time they are about seven years old.

It's a delicate subject because people don't like hearing that they're not going to change very much from the person they were at seven. But that's using the information in a negative way. I choose to use it in a positive way, telling people, "Be aware that you have a formidable challenge in altering who you were as a child. It's not going to happen easily. It's probably as difficult as trying to stop smoking. But if you accept it as a challenge, you have a far better opportunity to overcome it, to grow and to become the person you want to be."

Before we had a full-time recruiter, I did all of North Star's recruiting myself. As an example of our process, I'll share an actual case because it illustrates the potential impact of a psychological evaluation, the collective benefits of a correct evaluation and the eventual win-win result that can occur when recruiters faithfully follow a blueprint.

We had a young candidate, Mark McKasy, who was about to graduate from St. Thomas University. Mark went through our whole process and was approved all the way up to the psychologist — who recommended that we not extend Mark an offer because he was not a good fit for a sales career. I left a message for Mark to call me because I always made it a point never to give a candidate bad news over the phone. I thought they deserved better, having gone through such a thorough interview process. They deserved a counseling interview in which I shared with them positions or vocations they should consider.

So Mark returned the call and said, "How did I do?"

I replied, "Why don't you come in, and we'll talk about it."

"When do you want me to come in?" he asked excitedly.

"Well, how about ten tomorrow morning?"

It was then around noon, and he said, "I'll be there at ten tomorrow."

At 10:00 the following day, Mark appeared, and I proceeded to give him the bad news. I then told him what I thought he should be doing — something besides sales, because the psychologist had been quite emphatic about that.

Years later, I learned that Mark McKasy had been on a family vacation in Baltimore, Maryland, with his parents and two siblings when he made that call to me. His family aborted the vacation, jumped in the car and drove all night to get back to Minnesota just so Mark could come in for that 10:00 interview and get turned down for a career with us.

Ironically, Mark's father, Bert McKasy, later became the insurance commissioner for the state of Minnesota! You might imagine how concerned I became, knowing how upset he could have been with us and this firm for causing him and his entire family to drive all night, only to have his son turned down for a job. At that point, Bert would not have been my first choice for the person we'd want holding our fate in his hands.

It gets even more serendipitous. Today, Bert McKasy is a personal friend of mine, as well as North Star's attorney! We joke about this now but it wasn't funny at the time.

Mark McKasy is doing very well now, working in our industry in a back-office position and doing reinsurance work on commercial property and casualty lines. Sales clearly would have been a detour for him. A good selection system saved him precious time, and perhaps even more. Likewise, it spared us a hiring casualty.

Assets and Liabilities
Four questions I have been asking candidates since my Hartford days 40 years ago that have served us well are, "What would you consider your greatest personal asset? Your greatest personal liability? Your greatest business asset? Your greatest business liability?" By the latter two, I mean, "If you are extremely successful in 20 years, what characteristic do you have that may have made that success predictable? Likewise, if you don't achieve your highest ambitions, what characteristic do you have that may have been responsible for that shortfall?" I am always amazed at how forthright people are with their answers. Their answers provide an excellent opportunity to assess a candidate in a very short period of time.

Remember that the candidate and the firm are on the same side of the fence. If the firm mistakenly hires a candidate who later fails, both parties lose.

In 1977, I described this phenomenon in an article that I wrote for *Manager's Magazine,* published by LIMRA, titled "Is Putting Your Best Foot Forward Leaving Your Soul Behind?" The point of the article was that only complete disclosure and honesty on both sides in an interview can produce a mutually beneficial result. Deception by either party usually leads to catastrophic consequences for both. I believe that the concept was so novel 30 years ago that the piece won LIMRA's article-of-the-year award, and I was honored to meet George Joseph, LIMRA's CEO at the time, at their annual meeting to accept the honor. The concept is timeless.

The Big Four

Once you're fairly certain that you have found a candidate you want to hire, it's time to ask yourself the four big questions:

1. Would I be happy to take this person home to dinner and introduce him or her to my family?

2. If the CEO of my company walked in today, would I be very proud to introduce this person to him?

3. Would I be proud to walk this person around the whole company on the first day, introducing others to the newest member of our team?

4. If I had 20 other people lined up at my door for the same job and had only one position open, and I hadn't met the other 20 yet, would I still make this person that offer?

If I can answer "yes" to all of these questions, then this is the person I want.

All of these strategies support a simple but critical goal: to establish the culture of the organization and then hire to that culture.

Marginal Performers Contaminate Your Culture

Unfortunately, not every hire is a perfect hire. When you discover that a person you have hired is not having a positive impact on your organization or does not embrace your values, fire him quickly to minimize the negative effect he will have on your organization and the people in it. Malignancies generally spread; they rarely disappear.

No good can come of keeping a negative influence or a marginal performer in the job. Sometimes managers and general agents will reason, "Well, I've got the space anyway. I'll just keep this person around until a better one comes along." That's one of the cardinal mistakes you can make. Doing so will diminish the organization's esteem in the eyes of the other advisors, your team members and your strategic partners.

People like being around people who are successful. When you have hangers-on who are not ushered into other careers but who are allowed to stay, you contaminate your culture. The old cliché about a bad apple spoiling the barrel is valid. Further, by allowing that person to hang on, you may be keeping them from a rewarding career for which they are better suited. Kind management indeed is sometimes cruel management!

Keeping an office full because you happen to have empty space is fool's gold. You will pay for that folly in other ways — worst of all in the turnover of your good advisors, who may think, "Why do I want to be around here? This job is available to anybody. You don't have to perform to stay here." Mediocrity is contagious, just as success is. A high-performance culture must be just that.

Recycling People

A quarter-century ago, there was much talk about recycling paper. And the more I thought about recycling paper, the more it occurred to me that we should recycle people as well. After all, which is more important? I thought about what happens when advisors don't make it in our industry. The historical reaction is simply to fire them.

Jim Collins confirmed this recycling concept when he said that you can have the right person on the wrong seat on the bus. Sometimes you have quality people who just aren't meant to be advisors. They can't take the rejection, or they don't have the energy or the disposition or the resilience required to be an advisor. That in itself doesn't make them bad people, especially if the old axiom is right that only 2 percent of people can make it as advisors in our business. What do we do with them? Traditionally, we let them go.

I noticed this throughout my career, in different forms and in different companies. And then it occurred to me — if we have somebody who is really good but just not a good advisor, why don't we see if we can find another place for him or her in our home?

According to an article in *Business Week* magazine, 45 percent of young workers think it's a good idea for managers in a company to fire the bottom 10 percent of its performers each year. While this strategy might work for Jack Welch and General Electric, firing people across the board is not compatible with the sanctuary-like atmosphere that we want to create in our firm. That's why we hire selectively, provide extensive support to new advisors and consider recycling quality people who are not thriving in a particular role.

Dave Vasos, the chief financial officer of our company, has been with us for more than 25 years. He was hired as an advisor, but that was not the best role for his characteristics. Dave is a smart guy who has an M.B.A., with honors, from the University of Iowa. We therefore recycled him into the broker-dealer arena, where he performed with excellence. Today he is an indispensable member of our Corporate Development Council and a co-managing partner. Without Dave, North Star wouldn't be the firm it is today. The consequences of recycling can be far-reaching.

A similar situation happened with Ed Deutschlander, one of our executive vice presidents and managing partners. Ed left North Star because by the time he had been here for two years, he and his wife, Toni, had two children, and the income he was generating was insufficient for an entire family. To make ends meet, Ed took on a second job flipping burgers on a midnight shift. He was working the night shift there and then coming to North Star to work the "day shift." When I learned that he was working a second job, I questioned his actions — we do not want advisors who have only a part-time commitment to this career. Unfortunately, when Ed was informed of the policy, he didn't quit the night job as we expected; instead, he found it necessary to leave North Star. I didn't learn that he had left for two weeks. (Sometimes we delegate when we shouldn't!)

Diane Yohn, who is vice president of our Corporate Development Council and Client Services Division, reported that Ed had left. Realizing the mistake I had made, I immediately called him up and said, "Ed, what's going on?"

He said, "Phil, I had to make a difficult choice and for better or worse, made the one that was best for my family."

I said, "Ed, here's what I want you to do. I want you to hang up the phone, walk in to see your boss and tell him that a big mistake has been made, that you need to quit. Then I want you to come right back over here. We're going to find a position for you. But you're not leaving North Star. You're never leaving North Star." And he did it!

Clearly, it wasn't Ed's fault, but our own. We had him in the wrong market: the engineering-student market. Engineering students have no income. You can't have a primary breadwinner with children working in a market where the people don't have any income to compensate him. What is common knowledge now was unknown to us 15 years ago. We have since abandoned that market, but it was almost a very painful learning experience for us. North Star without Ed Deutschlander would be inconceivable.

There are several lessons here:

1. Loyal people will do things you ask of them, but only if you ask.
2. True talent is rare, and when found, simply must not be lost.
3. Never underestimate the esteem you as a leader possess with your team.

Chris Sitek is another example of our success in recycling good people. After he had succeeded for two years, Chris just quit. It was a Friday morning, and Shaun McDuffee (who heads our mentoring program, is on our Corporate Development Council and is now the regional vice president in our Austin office) and Ed Deutschlander both reported that Chris had turned in his resignation. He had reached that tipping point where he just couldn't face another rejection. He had used all of his resiliency and emotional strength to confront the constant rejection that is part of the early stage of this career. He had done it for as long as he could.

I remember saying, "He's a good man. Let's get him back in here and we'll find something for him to do."

Shaun or Ed replied, "He won't come back in."

I said, "Well, let's just get him back in anyway."

"No, you must understand that he is so downtrodden," they said. "This is the first thing in his life he's ever failed at." (Chris had been an honor student and a captain of the St. John's University football team.)

So I asked Ed and Shaun to join me in my office. Knowing that they are both very physically powerful guys, I asked, "Shaun, how big are you?"

He answered, "I'm six-four. Why?"

"How much do you weigh?"

Shaun answered quizzically, "About two-sixty-five, why?"

I said, "OK. Here's what I want you and Ed to do. On Monday morning, I want Chris in my office. I don't care if you have to kidnap him. I want him in my office at eight o'clock Monday morning. Are we clear?"

Both Shaun and Ed said, "Got it."

At 8:00 a.m. on Monday, Chris was sitting in the same chair that Shaun had sat in the previous Friday. I don't know how they did it, and quite frankly I'm glad I didn't ask them. I went through a recycling interview with Chris. We had talked about starting a brokerage company to handle all of our excess business. I began, "Chris, thanks for coming in. You're going to be our new brokerage manager. It's a new position that suits your high intellect, energy and needs." We shook hands, and the deal was done. That happened in 1998, and Chris has now built a brokerage agency that produced $1 million of premiums in 2006.

It is important to stay in touch with people and continue to let them know that they are welcome to come back. Jeff Landt was a successful advisor who had been with North Star for three years when he was offered a management position by the Securian broker-dealer division. After he spent three years in that role, we succeeded in hiring him back. He now leads our investment division with gross dealer concessions in excess of $11 million in 2006, and he has completed two-thirds of his CFA requirements.

If you get good people, stay with them. There's nothing new we're going to learn about Jeff Landt. We know who he is. We know he's got character, integrity, honor and energy. The two things we look for are energy and ethics — "E and E." If people have those, they should be recycled. If you don't have a position for them, think of creating one. Dave, Chris, Jeff and Ed, as well as some others, are at the epicenter of our success.

A few years ago, I made a presentation about recycling people at a meeting of the national managers of Principal Financial Group in Des Moines, Iowa. One of the managers in that group was an old GAMA friend named David Seems. David raised his hand in front of 60 fellow managers and said, "Phil, I heard you say that in a GAMA meeting a few years ago, so I tried it, and it worked for me, too." He went on to say that he had a female advisor who quit, and he called her back and said, "We want you to stay. You're going to head up our agency broker-dealer operation. You're going to manage our securities operation." Then he said, "Phil, she is one of the reasons why my agency is doing as great as it is today. It all happened because I heard your talk about recycling people, and I did it."

We have also kept quality people who no longer wanted to work in our main office. We have an advisor named Eric Seybert who came to us and said that he and his wife wanted to move back to their hometown of Bozeman, Montana. He told me, "We don't want to live in a big metropolitan area anymore. We'd rather raise our children in a more rural area. Danielle and I have decided we want to move back to Bozeman. But I still want to keep my clients." He moved back to Montana three years ago, and his production has not suffered. He does all of his work with his physician clients, who are in many different cities all over the country, through the Internet. If we had had a one-size-fits-all organization or policy, we would be without Eric today.

High-quality people who support and contribute to your culture are a special find. If you hire someone who is perfect for your organization in every way except for the job that they're in, look for a way to recycle them. If you don't have a position for them, try to create one.

> *Every person you hire has to have integrity, intelligence and maturity. Once you have those, look for the four Es — positive energy, the ability to energize others, edge (the ability to make tough yes-or-no decisions) and the ability to execute — and for passion.*
>
> JACK WELCH

You Take the Helm

- **Hire Slowly** — Take your time to carefully select quality people who will make a positive impact on your organization. Culture matters!

- **Determine if Your Candidate Is a Natural Optimist** — People don't change much after the age of seven. One way to find out if someone has a positive attitude is to ask about their earliest memories and look for positive answers.

- **Fire Quickly** — If a person you've hired is having a negative impact on your organization or does not embrace your values, fire them quickly.

- **Recycle People** — If a quality person is not excelling in the position you hired him for, try to find him a new role that is a better match with his personality and skill set.

- **Realize that "One Size Fits All" Is Outdated** — Expand your business model to the realities of today. Design one that keeps good people instead of losing them out the back door.

Chapter 4

Cop, Coach, Community
From Autocracy to Interdependence

JOHN LEFFERTS, a very successful manager from AXA Equitable, delivered a general session presentation at LAMP 1994 where, for the first time, I learned the "Cop, Coach, Consultant" concept of working with advisors. I have heard many compelling presentations at LAMP, but this was one of the very best.

In 2004, North Star revised this strategy by replacing "consultant" with "community." This is more in line with our philosophy of "You are in business *for* yourself but not *by* yourself." Further, it better represents our familial atmosphere of caring and our collective efforts of giving back to our neighborhoods, communities and the North Star family.

These three words, placed in the right order — cop, coach, community — provide field leaders with a simple game plan, not only for understanding the process of growing advisors, but also for enhancing the selection process. Our business is difficult enough to succeed in; those uncoachable individuals who fight the system simply stack the odds further against themselves. On the other hand, people who have faith in the system increase their probability of success.

We have always known that we must interact with seasoned, successful advisors differently from how we interact with new advisors. The cop, coach, community approach to management helps field leaders understand this progression of career development and describes the type of support that we, as managers, should be providing at each point during our advisors' careers.

The Cop Stage

Success is rarely possible without discipline. During the cop stage, management must observe the self-discipline level of the new advisor. Discipline can come from within a person or from without — and both sources work.

The U.S. Marine Corps is proof that external discipline works. Marines don't always come to the table with discipline, but you can bet it will be provided once they enlist. Our training program is similar. We provide the discipline to hold advisors accountable for as long as it is needed, typically for a minimum of 90 days.

We have found that the following concepts are critical to success during the cop stage of advisor development. You will find more detail about each concept in the chapter noted.

Concept	Chapter
Critical Number	8
Habits	14
20,000 Rejections	15
High-Performance, No-Excuse Culture	21
Expect What You Inspect	23

The discipline and structure that you administer during the cop phase is absolutely critical to a new advisor's success. But equally critical is letting the advisor advance to the coach phase at the appropriate time. This is easier said than done and is quite similar to the challenge that most parents face in gradually "letting go" as our children mature.

This is a very delicate issue. Many managers continue to keep people in the cop stage, and that can be a prescription for disaster and for losing them. We have lost people that way ourselves. At some point, you must let them go. You have to show them the loyalty and respect that says that you trust them to exercise the self-discipline to do the right things. Most will give the loyalty and respect right back to you by doing the right things.

Sometimes we are able to let advisors leave the cop phase before their initial 90-day training period is over because they're exercising all kinds of self-discipline, doing everything that we ask them to do and more. We don't ask people to come into the office on Saturdays and Sundays. But here they are. If somebody is giving you that kind of effort, you don't have to be their cop anymore. But they do still need coaching, direction, support and nurturing. You will provide that to them during the coach stage.

The Coach Stage

Wrestlers and other athletes start out doing a lot of physical conditioning and learning the basics of their sport. But as they advance, they need a coach to help them build and refine their individual skills and talents. Advisors are much the same. Once they learn the fundamentals of the career and begin to demonstrate discipline, they no longer need a cop. At that point in their development, they need a coach to help them build their skills, and that is what members of management must be prepared to become. Coaches dictate the rules of engagement for advisors — meetings, reports, compliance, drills, presentations and the like.

We have found that the following concepts are critical to success during the coach stage of advisor development. You will find more detail about each concept in the chapter noted.

Concept	Chapter
Life Insurance Focus	10
Written Goals	13
Mentoring Culture	18
Study Groups	19
Coach, Don't Coax	20
Quarterly Reviews	22

This second stage lasts until advisors hit our minimum level of acceptable production, Million Dollar Round Table (MDRT). Then, although they may no longer need a coach, we will act in that capacity if that is their choice. The usual transition, however, is for advisors to move from the coach stage into the community stage.

The Community Stage

Before advisors qualify for MDRT, which is our firm's break-even revenue point, they are our customers and our dependents, and they operate under our autocracy. Then, once they hit MDRT, they become our partners — consultants who function interdependently with our firm.

This is a critical turning point. If our attitude toward that person does not recognize his or her contributions to the firm, then the firm is vulnerable to that successful advisor seeking alternatives elsewhere. Reaching the MDRT milestone represents the point when the very autocratic system that successfully guided that advisor from novice to accomplished practitioner must evolve also.

We have found that the following concepts are critical to success during the community stage of advisor development. You will find more detail about each concept in the chapter noted.

Concept	Chapter
Do What You're Best At, Delegate the Rest	5
Leaders Are Teachers	6
Servant Leadership	7
Creativity and Relationships	9
Specialize	11
Blended, Not Balanced	12
Your Worst Deal Is Your Only Deal	16
The 80–20 Rule	17
Live Where You Want, With Those You Love, Doing the Right Work, On Purpose	24
Live your Legacy	25

This is a healthy outcome, with all parties operating in an adult, mutually respectful, growing relationship. No parents, no children. Love, respect and a sense of community replace a directive and nurturing, parent-knows-best environment.

A Guide for Managers

In the book *Leadership and the One-Minute Manager*[1] the authors outline four basic leadership styles that mirror the cop, coach, community approach. Their directing style corresponds with our cop phase, their coaching and supporting styles correspond with our coach phase, and their delegating style corresponds with our community phase.

The authors explain that there is no one best leadership style. Rather, managers should match their leadership style with the appropriate developmental level of the person they are working with on a situational basis.

The authors describe the leader's role in each of the leadership styles, as follows.

---

[1] Kenneth Blanchard, Ph.D.; Patricia Zigarmi, Ed.D.; and Drea Zitgarmi, Ed.D., *Leadership and the One-Minute Manager: Increasing Effectiveness Through Situational Leadership*, William Morrow and Company, Inc., New York, 1985.

Directing Style (corresponds with cop phase)
In this phase, the leader provides specific direction and closely monitors task accomplishment.

Coaching Style (corresponds with coach phase)
In this phase, the leader continues to direct and closely monitor task accomplishment but also explains decisions, solicits suggestions and supports progress.

Supporting Style (also corresponds with coach phase)
In this phase, the leader facilitates and supports efforts toward task accomplishment and shares responsibility for decision making.

Delegating Style (corresponds with community phase)
In this phase, the leader turns over responsibility for decision making and problem solving to the individual.

Cop, Coach, Community as a Selection Tool

The cop, coach, community process is an excellent selection tool. It serves as one of the best pain killers a firm can deploy. We've all hired that promising recruit who we soon discovered thought he had all the answers and was simply uncoachable. And the compassionate leader privately sighs, "Here we go again." It has happened to us, too. It is a punishing experience, both emotionally and financially, for a field leader to hire someone who is not coachable.

Make Your Interviews Structured but Flexible

The failure of advisors with that kind of attitude is predictable. If you hammer on the cop, coach, community approach in the interview process, you can weed out those who find that approach unacceptable. As you repeat the process over and over during your selection interviews, you'll find out quickly which recruits consider the cop phase to be offensive because they know it will require them to subordinate their egos and accept authority. It becomes a self-selection device with the candidates disqualifying us for their own reasons.

A good example of how this interview process works occurred with one of our perennial Court of the Table qualifiers, Marshall W. Gifford, CLU ChFC. During our interview with Marshall in 1993, I learned that he had played varsity basketball on a full scholarship for three years. When I asked him what happened in his senior year, he answered that he had quit the team and given his scholarship back after his junior year.

Did I have an authority-resentment issue on my hands? That question became the main focus for the remainder of the interview. I proceeded to ask questions such as, "What adjectives would you use to describe your high school football coach? What adjectives would you use to describe your high school teachers?" I asked the same about additional authority figures from his past. Fortunately, every single one of them elicited positive descriptions from Marshall. His basketball coach turned out to be the only authority figure that had ever been a problem for him. Later I learned that others had had similar experiences with the same coach. And it turned out that Marshall was such an outstanding athlete that he went on to his college track team the next year without a scholarship and finished seventh in the nation in the decathlon!

Marshall was extremely coachable and today is not only a valuable senior advisor, but one of the finest mentors I have been privileged to know. He has since co-written a financial planning book for dentists with another of our advisors, Todd Bramson.

A highly structured interview that lacked flexibility could have cost us an unbelievable candidate who is now an extremely valuable part of North Star's culture and team. This next story demonstrates just how valuable Marshall is to us and to his clients.

In May 2003, Marshall met with a young couple who were his clients; they were both dentists in their late 20s. During his review with them, Marshall discussed life insurance, and they applied to increase their coverage to $2 million. Because the husband had had some minor health issues, underwriting resulted in a standard rating rather than the preferred offer they were expecting. This caused the premium to be significantly more expensive than they had hoped it would be. After some discussions between Marshall and the couple, it was decided that, for the short-term, the policy would be issued at $1 million until the husband was settled in his dental practice. The couple hesitated about writing the check because the premium was higher, but Marshall emphasized the importance of getting the coverage in place. In July 2003, the couple submitted the check to bind the $1 million of coverage.

Only five weeks later, just before the husband was to begin practice, he found out that he had Stage IV lung cancer. He and his wife had a two-year-old child and a second child on the way. He was only 29 years old and had never smoked. Of course it was devastating news.

Throughout the next seven months, Marshall's client underwent treatments, went on disability and then died in May 2004. He had paid the life insurance company a total of $83, which resulted in a death claim of more than $1 million. Marshall has commented numerous times about how difficult it was for him to deal with this heartbreaking situation, but also how thankful he was to be able to help this family.

Before the client passed away, he mentioned to Marshall how thankful he was that Marshall had made sure that his policy was in place. He told Marshall how much easier it was for him, even though he was dying, to know that he had done what a husband and father should do by taking care of his family's finances.

After the client died, the man's widow contacted Marshall and thanked him several times for making sure that they were covered. The most profound and touching note that Marshall received from the widow came with a picture of her one- and three-year-old sons with a note that said, "Marshall, I wanted you to have a picture of my boys. Thank you for making their future comfortable and secure."

Imagine what our firm and this family would have lost if I had not delved more deeply in our initial interview into the reasons why

Marshall appeared to have a resentment of authority. It's important enough to say again: Conduct highly structured interviews, but be sure to build in enough flexibility to let the interview go where the ebb and flow take you. If something doesn't sound right, ask a lot of questions.

Because of the importance of the coachability issue, we now require new recruits to sign a statement that outlines these requirements before we hire them. (This statement is included in the Appendix.) So if a recruit says he agrees to abide by the principles outlined in the cop, coach, community process but later has a change of heart about the cop phase, we have a point of reference to guide him back to.

The Three I's

During the recruiting process, we're looking for people who are malleable. We've found that people who understand and respond to what we call "the three I's" — impact, independence and income — tend to be coachable. We're looking for young people who want to come into this business because they want to have an *impact* on the lives of their fellow man. Impact is the most important of the three I's. Number two is that they will serve their fellow man in an *independent* manner, once they've advanced out of the "cop" and "coach" phases. They won't have to ask us when they can play golf once they're successful. The third concept we go through in the interview is that their *income* potential will be similar to that of a physician if they follow our guidance in the beginning and succeed in this business.

We had one young advisor who almost didn't make it but who finally pulled through. He had been a football captain in college and came from extremely humble beginnings. When he entered our program, he was highly suspicious of everything — our system, our management's motives — because he had never been in a warm, familial relationship outside of his home. After six months, we considered asking him to leave. He just wasn't part of the culture.

Then he had an epiphany: "The reason they are being so hard on me is that they want to help me, and they told me that at the beginning." He began responding to the support and concern of the people who were in charge of his career and success. In his second calendar year here, he qualified as an MDRT aspirant. The transformation was simply amazing, and thereafter he was aligned with our values 100 percent. Fortunately he had the maturity and wisdom to recognize the truth.

In Chapter 22, we talk about the "big why" that motivates people to achieve their goals. When I asked this young man what his "big why" was — why he reached his goal of becoming an MDRT aspirant — he answered, "My parents have always lived in a trailer. I wanted to buy them a house." That personal goal motivated him to succeed and helped him realize that the discipline we provided to him early in his career was actually helping him achieve his goal and become successful in this business.

From Autocracy to Interdependence

Author Stephen Covey describes a "maturity continuum" that spans from dependence to independence to interdependence. He says that interdependence is the paradigm of "we" and is the most mature, advanced concept of the three. He explains that interdependent people have the opportunity to share themselves deeply and meaningfully with others and have access to the vast resources and potential of other human beings. But he also says that interdependence is a choice that only *independent* people can make. *Dependent* people cannot choose to become *interdependent*. They don't have the character to do it, and they don't own enough of themselves.[2] I would add that they don't have the self-confidence to become interdependent either, since interdependence requires you to place your future in another's hands, even if only temporarily.

---

[2]Stephen R. Covey, *The 7 Habits of Highly Effective People: Powerful Lessons in Personal Change*, Simon & Schuster, New York, 1989, pp. 48-49, 51.

Covey's explanation illustrates the cop, coach, community theory well. Advisors start out by depending on those who are guiding their growth. Then they assume more responsibility and become more independent. Finally, they advance to the stage where they make optimal use of their personal resources and the resources of the firm that originally guided them. But they cannot become interdependent until they first progress through the other two phases. The continuum is the key to advisors becoming partners in our collective success.

It is the field leader's role and privilege to guide them through that process.

> *Discipline without freedom is tyranny.*
> *Freedom without discipline is chaos.*
> CULLEN HIGHTOWER

You Take the Helm

- **Hire Coachable Advisors** — Use the "cop, coach, community" concept as a selection tool. Explain to candidates that new advisors will be subject to an autocratic environment characterized by strict accountability and discipline during their first 90 days. If they have concerns about this arrangement, they probably are not coachable and should look elsewhere.

- **Let Advisors Advance** — Once advisors have mastered the requirements of a given stage, let them advance to the next stage. Be prepared to assume a different role with them.

- **Be a Cop in the Beginning** — Direct all aspects of your advisors' activities during their first 90 days. Show, teach and require them to perform the activities that are necessary to succeed in the business.

- **Become a Coach** — Coach your advisors in the use of the tools that will move them to the next level in their development. Everyone needs a coach.

- **In the Final Stage, Treat Them Like Partners** — When advisors have reached the standards you have established for them to be considered partners, grant them the freedom that only the community stage permits. They will demonstrate respect and loyalty to you and will come to be partners in your collective success.

Author's Note

In recent years, many advisors have acknowledged the need for accountability and help by hiring, at great expense, personal coaches. Emerson said it best: "What I need is someone who will make me do what I can."

The quarterly review, which we discuss in Chapter 22, is a firm's value-added way of helping advisors avoid paying for outside consultants or coaches. It is a key tactic for adding value for your advisors. It is an important element in demonstrating your understanding that your advisors are your customers and that this is a critical "deliverable" to them.

I am often asked whether personal coaches are good or bad. Surely there are times when coaches can be effective. Nonetheless, I have always viewed it as somewhat of a personal failure when an advisor retains an outside coach. Coaching is my job. That's what I do.

Granted, coaching does not come naturally to some managers. There are many resources to draw on for help, however. For example, a recently published book, *The Power of Coaching ... Engaging in Excellence* (ProBrilliance Leadership Institute, 2007), is one. This is a collaborative effort of top field leaders and executive coaches in the industry. It describes what it takes to affect others profoundly and inspire lasting growth and change. Books such as *The Power of Coaching* can take your coaching game to the next level.

Although I do believe that using an outside coach can sometimes be of value, the coach-manager model is more effective simply because of the differences between the end goals of the advisor and the external coach. Typically, advisors want to fix a problem — accelerate their growth curve, catapult their career or otherwise accomplish a quantum leap forward in their practice and be done with it. Many times the external coach is looking for an annuity. At the end of each engagement, the coach needs to prospect again to replace that client.

As internal coaches, we have the same goals as our advisors. We want to help them grow and move on to a new level. That is why we now use "community" instead of "consultant" in our three Cs. It places the focus on the bigger picture — the collective good of the North Star family — instead of on the individual.

Chapter 5

Chinese Table Tennis

Do What You're Best At; Delegate the Rest

WHEN I WRESTLED in high school and college, I was a "counter-wrestler": I wasn't fast enough for a strong offensive approach, but I was quick to react defensively. My strategy was to wait for my opponent to make a mistake and then capitalize on it by making a counter-move against him. I knew I'd never be fast, so I didn't waste time trying to become faster. Instead, I honed my defensive skills to make them even stronger.

This concept applies to management and leadership, too. I've always believed that you get far better results by focusing on the kind of work you're good at and delegating the work that you're not good at to someone else.

One day in 1973, I gave a presentation on this very concept to a group of John Hancock managers in Atlanta, Georgia. The presentation was titled "The Art of Management in an Age of Uncertainty," and I had been giving it to various industry groups for many years. In the presentation, I advised managers to find out what they really loved doing and then backfill the things they didn't like to do by hiring people who were good at those things.

My contact at John Hancock was a regional vice president named Roy DiLiberto, who later became the first president of the Financial Planning Association. Roy and I had attended Temple University together. At a cocktail party after my presentation, Roy said, "You know, Phil, the subject of your presentation is the philosophy behind an article I recently read about Chinese table tennis."

That piqued my interest, and I asked him to tell me about it.

According to the article, South Korea dominated table tennis in the mid-20th century. But at the world championships, the Chinese fielded a team at the international level for the first time ever, and they didn't just beat the Koreans in the finals; they embarrassed them.

After the tournament, a sportswriter from the United States approached the coach of the Chinese table tennis team and asked, "How did you do that?"

"It's very easy," the coach replied. "We practice eight hours a day."

The writer said, "Come on, now. Everybody here practices at least eight hours a day. There must be more to it than that."

The coach said, "We practice differently. You see, we only practice the things we're good at, and we ignore the things that we don't do well. So if we have a player who wins a regional table tennis championship in Guang Dong Province and makes it to the nationals because she has a strong serve, we focus on improving her serve and not her weak backhand. We believe that if we can make her strengths strong enough, her weaknesses will not matter."

What an epiphany! It was exactly what I had been talking about for years. Now I had a compelling metaphor that I could share to illustrate this important concept.

I recently read another story that reaffirmed my belief in this concept. Jim Kaat, a pitcher for the Minnesota Twins, traced his success back to spring training in 1966. That's when the team's new pitching coach, Johnny Sain, watched his pitchers perform and then asked them what they thought their strengths were, from strongest to weakest. Kaat told Sain that his fastball was his best pitch, followed by his curve, and his slider and changeup were his weakest pitches.

"What pitch do you spend the most time practicing?" Sain asked, and Kaat replied that he practiced his slider and changeup the most. Sain asked him to take a different approach. "Work on your fastball. I know it's your favorite pitch, so go out there in practice, warm-ups and during games, and concentrate on your fastball. Throw your fastball 80 to 90 percent of the time all year, and you'll win a lot of ball games."

Kaat left Sain's office stunned and a little disappointed that the coach didn't provide him with advice for smoothing out his curveball. But that season, Kaat took Sain's advice, throwing so many fastballs that he said he thought his arm was going to fall off. That year, Kaat won 26 games and went on to become Pitcher of the Year in the American League.[1]

Identify Your Strengths; Backfill the Rest

These stories let me make my point to field leaders that if you're not the best recruiter in the world, don't worry about it — just hire a good recruiter. But if you love recruiting and you're good at it, then keep doing it. Figure out what you don't like to do and aren't good at, and hire someone to handle that area of your business. If you continue to work on the things you're best at — trying to be the best in the world — you'll build a successful firm. If you keep trying to develop gifts you don't have, you'll be far less efficient and effective at taking your organization to the next level.

In the complex world of the field manager, there are many critical functions. Some managers are very good at detail work and, consequently, might make terrific compliance officers, market-conduct people or chief financial officers in their firms. Others who are not very detail-oriented (and I would guess that includes most of

---

[1] Leo Hauser, *Leo Hauser's Five Steps to Success*, Hauser Productions: Wayzata, Minn., 1993, as cited in Glenn Van Ekeren, *Speaker's Sourcebook II*, Penguin Putnam Inc., New York, 1994, p. 7.

us in this business) should be spending the majority of our time using our people skills with our firms' teams and our clients. We should hire to the jobs we're not proficient at, which may be budgeting, administration, underwriting, communications with the home office, policy service — all the tasks that require refined skills for detail work versus people skills.

This concept is somewhat counterintuitive. It's human nature for people to try to work on their areas of weakness instead of delegating them to someone else. This is especially true of competitors, and field leaders generally come from the ranks of successful advisors, who are by nature competitors. They're warriors, and warriors want to win. Whatever they're not good at, they'll keep working at. So when successful advisors become managers, their competitive nature makes them want to work on the things they're not very good at. The advice I give them is the opposite: Do the things you're really good at, and backfill with other people to do the things you don't like to do or that require skills you're not blessed with.

I believe that most managers have better people skills than detail skills. But most of them spend an equal amount of time — or maybe even more time — on detail work, when they really ought to be hiring somebody else to do that.

Advisors Need to Backfill, Too

If you carry this idea to its logical conclusion, it's one of the best supervisory tools a field leader can have because it applies to advisors as well as managers. As leaders, we set either a good example or a bad example. The function of a field leader is to help advisors build and improve their practices and take them to the next level. Advisors have the same challenge managers do: They try to be all things to all people, to do everything themselves.

I've found that the more productive advisors are, the more they tend to be perfectionists. They dot their i's and cross their t's, and they insist on doing their own proposals and other detail work that they really don't have the time or skills for. Advisors come into this business because they love working with people. But often the more successful they become, the less time they spend with people. The rule about working on your strengths instead of your weaknesses tells us not to let that happen. It tells our advisors to continue to spend as much time as possible in front of people and to build their staffs around the skill sets required for the other tasks. For instance, an advisor who is not very good on the phone should look for an administrative assistant who has good phone skills for setting up appointments and reviews.

Advisors need to backfill to compensate for their weaknesses in much the same way that managers do.

Because firms today are so much larger and more complex than they were several decades ago, there is more opportunity for field leaders and advisors to delegate to others the tasks that are not their forte.

How Good Would Mickey Mantle Really Be?

When I was a high school wrestler, a lot of the kids on the team smoked. My wrestling coach would yell at them for smoking, and they'd fire back with, "Yeah, well, Mickey Mantle smokes."

I'll never forget my wrestling coach's response: "Yes, but how good would Mickey Mantle *really* be?"

I have an advisor who is a perennial Court of the Table producer, and I would like to take him to Top of the Table. His Achilles heel is that he's a perfectionist. I hired him in 1976. For the past 30 years, when we've gotten together for our quarterly, semiannual or annual reviews, we come back to the same place: He's such a perfectionist. He has a staff of six administrative and marketing assistants. He gives them assignments and then goes over their work with a fine-tooth comb. I say to him, "Why don't you fire that person? You're doing all the work a second time anyway."

You must hire people you trust, then you must empower them. They may make a mistake or two that you wouldn't make, but you can't be so meticulous that you're going to continue to second-guess them on every detail. If they perform 100 tasks and make two mistakes where you might have made only one mistake, you have to measure the cost of doing 100 things yourself just to correct one mistake. It's highly inefficient.

The opportunity cost of that approach is that advisors are missing valuable chances to build their practices. So coach your advisors to find people who are good at administrative tasks but may make two mistakes instead of one, recognizing that from time to time the advisor may have to apologize to someone and accept responsibility for a team member's mistake.

My perfectionist advisor is very successful — he makes almost half a million dollars a year. But if he focused on what he's good at and delegated the rest — if he removed the obstacle that's getting in the way of even greater success — how good could he *really* be?

Frank Sinatra Doesn't Move Pianos

I heard this story about Frank Sinatra some time ago. It is another excellent example of why doing what you're best at and delegating the rest is so important.

In the early 1970s, a soldier came back from Vietnam, where Frank Sinatra had performed for the troops. An acquaintance asked this soldier, "You mean you really met Frank Sinatra?" He said, "Yes, I did. Many times."

"Well, what's he like?"

"Frank Sinatra doesn't move pianos," the soldier replied. "That's what he's like. He has someone bring the piano in, set it up and tune it. He sits down, plays the piano and sings, and then he gets up, takes a bow and walks away."

Managers and advisors must think about their practice the same way: Don't move pianos. Do the things that are going to get you the applause — spend your time with people. That's where your skills are. That's where you're the most highly efficient. If you're going to do $20-an-hour work, you're going to get paid $20 an hour. If you want to make $400 an hour, do $400-an-hour work, which is spending time in front of people — not moving pianos.

Having lower-paid team members "move pianos" makes good business sense. In *The E Myth Revisited*, Michael Gerber recommends having every function in the company done by the person who has the lowest level of skill necessary to fulfill the intended function[2]. That allows you to create a model that is transferable. You can replicate the model because you don't have people who are overpaid or overqualified performing functions that others could do. It lets you build what Gerber calls a "systems-dependent" business rather than a "people-dependent" or "expert-dependent" business.

One of our advisors has already qualified for Top of the Table at 27 years old. He qualified for Court of the Table three years in a row and has qualified for Million Dollar Round Table every year since he came into the business. He doesn't move pianos.

He does joint fieldwork. He doesn't do any prospecting, but he's a tremendous closer. He's great in front of people. He's a good advanced underwriter. He knows that he is most effective when he's in front of people, so he has positioned himself with all the new people in the firm as a joint-fieldwork person, the one who can close cases and help them succeed.

He leaves his appointment book on his desk, and the newer advisors just come in and fill in appointments for people they're bringing in — people they would never have the confidence to even call on if they were going to do it by themselves. This advisor will convince those people that we really know what we're doing, and he will close the case. This setup has benefited him personally, too — it helped him make Top of the Table at an early age.

Yes, the system works, and he is only one of many examples of how well it works.

Another example is Shaun McDuffee. I offered Shaun a general agent position in Austin, Texas, and he declined. "I don't want to move pianos," he said. "I want to make Top of the Table every year, and I want to grow people. If I became a general agent, I'd have to do too many other things that would keep me from making Top of the Table and growing people."

A wise man, that Shaun.

---

[2]Michael E. Gerber, *The E Myth Revisited: Why Most Small Businesses Don't Work and What to Do About It,* HarperCollins Publishers, New York, 2001, p. 100.

Let Physicians Focus on Medicine

Physicians don't want to move pianos — or build their own financial plans. They are extremely smart people. You have to be extremely smart to get into medical school, let alone to get out of one with a degree. These are bright people, and almost all of them could do financial planning if they wanted to — maybe not the selling part, but the detail part, the mathematical part, the Monte Carlo part. Their IQs are high enough to do that. But that's not what they want to do. They want to practice medicine. You might say, "Yes, but physicians can go on the Internet, come up with financial programs, and save the hourly fees a financial planner will charge them." But they don't want to do it. They're smart enough, but that's not how they want to spend their time. They'd rather make $400 an hour doing the things that are more in line with their skill set and their passion.

Greater Success Through Synergy

Steven Covey's concept of interdependence is a good model for building an effective, synergistic team, with each member of the team responsible for the tasks that he or she is good at.[3]

We have a team of three young people who have a shared practice in one of our offices. All three are Round Table qualifiers, and one is a Court of the Table qualifier. One guy is a rainmaker. He loves people, and he loves bringing people in the front door. The second guy was failing out of the business but is a highly skilled technician. I would lovingly call him a geek because he loves numbers, and he's good at them. He likes people, but his people skills aren't as good as the first guy's are. The third guy on the team, my Court of the Table producer, loves being in interviews. He was a book salesman in college. He loves just showing up, spending time with people and showing them where life insurance fits into their financial program and where risk management is in their best interest. He's a closer.

---

[3]Stephen R. Covey, *The 7 Habits of Highly Effective People: Powerful Lessons in Personal Change*, Simon & Schuster, New York, 1989, pp. 185–203.

These three people with different skill sets have teamed up. All three have increased their production immensely because each one is doing a part of the process rather than trying to be everything to everybody. Each advisor has found his fastball.

People are happier when they're doing what they're good at, and that happiness fuels success. If you do the things you're good at and that you love doing and delegate the rest, going to work is a joy, and you enhance your own existence and the quality of life of all the other people in the office who see how much you enjoy doing what you're doing. The smile on your face, the graciousness with which you carry yourself and your enthusiasm for your work are infectious.

I tell others, "If you're not having fun, you're not doing it right."

> *A man who loves what he is doing will never work another day in his life.*
>
> CONFUCIUS

You Take the Helm

- **Play to Your Strengths** — Develop the skills you enjoy. If you're the best at one thing, you can have anything.

- **Backfill Your Weak Points** — Hire to complement your talents with those you're not blessed with. Resist the temptation to be like the guy who bought a new boomerang and spent the rest of his life trying to throw the old one away.

- **Coach Your Advisors to Do the Same** — Competitive people, such as advisors, tend to work on their areas of weakness. As Sam Rayburn, former speaker of the House of Representatives, used to say, "There's no education in the second kick of a mule." Help advisors understand that when they're building their practices, it's important for them to hire people to do the things they're not good at themselves.

- **Delegate Tasks to Appropriate Levels of Expertise** — Assign each task to the person who has the lowest level of skill necessary to get the required results. Empower them.

- **Move Pianos for the Professionals** — Financial planners have a tremendous opportunity in our very complex financial world, because other professionals don't want to "move pianos" or build their own financial plans.

- **Maximize Synergy** — Form teams of individuals who have different skill sets so that each task is performed by someone who excels in that area. Then your advisors can do what they enjoy doing and are good at instead of trying to be everything to everybody. That's when everyone will have fun.

Chapter 6

Leading Through Teaching

I BELIEVE THAT all true leaders are teachers as well as world-class learners. They are devoted to lifelong learning.

Some teachers are more vocal about their message and share their knowledge with the masses rather than with just a few, but all true leaders dedicate their lives to growing other people through the transfer of knowledge.

Every winning organization that I've seen, whether at the firm level or the company level, is a teaching-focused organization, almost like a university campus. A big part of its culture is developing people.

The greatest leaders are people who have a strong set of values. We may not always agree with them, but these leaders have values that they've developed into a culture, and they energize others on the basis of those values, through teaching.

The three best teachers I've read about are Mahatma Ghandi, Martin Luther King Jr. and Jesus of Nazareth. We still have their ideas and values with us today because they were so effective in communicating them to other people — their disciples. The disciples learned from the masters and taught others, and that process continues, thus preserving their legacy.

What these three leaders taught was not always popular at the time they were teaching it. They had what Jack Welch, the former CEO of General Electric, called "edge." *Edge* is the ability to fire your own brother if he's not performing. It's the conviction and courage to say, "I have a job to do, and I want to enlist your help to do it; but if you choose a different path, I can't have you with me."

One of my favorite examples of leadership through teaching is from a book called *Sacred Hoops*[1] by Phil Jackson. Jackson was the head coach of the Chicago Bulls from 1989 to 1998 and head coach of the LA Lakers from 1999 through 2004 and again since 2005.

When Michael Jordan joined the NBA with Chicago in 1984, he was probably the best player who ever came off a college campus — maybe the best player of all time. Phil Jackson couldn't teach Michael Jordan much about basketball, so he focused on honing Jordan's leadership skills. He asked him to begin sharing the spotlight with his teammates so they could grow. Jordan replied, "Okay. You know me: I've always been a coachable player. Whatever you want to do, I'm behind you."[2]

In *Michael Jordan Speaks: Lessons from the World's Greatest Champion*, author Janet Lowe says, "Coach Phil Jackson viewed the early Michael Jordan as 'a Michelangelo in baggy shorts,' a stellar player who, nevertheless, had not quite mastered the art of team leadership. Under Jackson's guidance, Jordan began to see himself as a player with the ability to influence others."[3]

Although Michael Jordan forfeited many points in NBA games because he began sharing the ball more, he never resented it because he continued to achieve tremendous success. In fact, Jordan stated many times that he would never play for any coach except Jackson.[4]

---

[1] Phil Jackson and Hugh Delehanty, *Sacred Hoops: Spiritual Lessons of a Hardwood Warrior*, Hyperion Books, New York, 1995.
[2] Ibid., p. 101.
[3] Janet Lowe, *Michael Jordan Speaks: Lessons from the World's Greatest Champion*, John Wiley & Sons, Inc., New York, 1999, p. 38.
[4] Ibid., p. 180.

As field leaders, we have the privilege and responsibility to recognize and channel the talents of our superstars to achieve optimum benefit for everyone involved — themselves, their fellow advisors, our firms and agencies and our clients.

Teachable Moments

Not every opportunity to teach will be as big or as obvious as the Michael Jordan example. As leaders, we must look for teachable moments everywhere.

Our Portland, Oregon, office opened for business on October 1, 2004. On my first visit there, I met the receptionist. After we talked for a few minutes, I asked her, "What's your job?"

"I'm the receptionist," she replied.

"Do you know what you really are?"

"No," she said hesitantly.

"You are the director of first impressions," I said. I explained that her job was not just answering the phone or greeting people, but that she truly was the first impression clients and applicants had of our company when they walked through the door. I was teaching her how important her role is.

The next time I walked into that office, I greeted her and asked, "Hey, what's your job?"

"I'm the director of first impressions," she said confidently.

Jack Welch was part of my inspiration for the conversations I had with our Portland receptionist. He used a method called "management by walking around" or MBWA. He would walk around and talk to his employees, without regard for their role or status in the company. This was not a quick task, because GE was a huge organization, with close to 300,000 employees in 1985.

As he walked around engaging his employees in conversation, Welch used a tactic known as the Socratic method. He would ask them question after question — what their job was, how they felt about it, what they liked most and least about it, how their job functions fit in with the bigger goal and vision of the company and how they felt about that connection. If employees didn't have a clear understanding about how their job connected with the company's overall mission, he would teach them.

Leading Through Learning

Good leaders know that you can't rise to be the best in any profession if you're not growing and learning all the time. The world is changing quickly. If you're using yesterday's weapons to fight tomorrow's battles, you're going to be ill-equipped to deal with all the changes society is bringing our way. And the speed of change continues to accelerate. To get ahead of the curve, we must constantly sharpen our tools and our mental faculties, as well as our awareness of what's going on in the world around us.

Leaders can learn by asking a lot of questions, reading, observing other successful people and using situation recognition.

Asking a Lot of Questions

Jack Welch wasn't just teaching while he walked around asking questions. He was also learning. Asking questions was Welch's way of finding out more about his company. He was getting information directly from his employees, not filtered or altered by someone else. Welch is an example of a great leader. Largely because of his influence, GE has produced more CEOs for Fortune 500 companies than any other single organization in America.

Navy Captain Mike Abrashoff used the same technique when he was the commander of the *USS Benfold*. In his LAMP 2006 general session presentation, Abrashoff explained that he interviewed every sailor on the ship to build personal relationships with them and encourage them to make more of a contribution to the ship's success. He said it's important to ask questions of employees, to listen aggressively and to empower them to suggest improvements. He gave an example of a sailor who, when finally asked the right question, made an excellent suggestion that saved the ship time, money and manpower. When Captain Abrashoff interviewed the sailor to find out more about him and his work, the young man talked about how, because of the constant rusting of the ferrous-metal nuts and bolts that lined the sides of the ship, sailors had to spend entire days sanding down rust and had to repaint the ship six times a year. He suggested that they use stainless steel nuts and bolts instead. Abrashoff implemented the suggestion, which kept the crew from having to paint the ship for nearly a year. Now the entire Navy has adopted stainless steel fasteners for installation on every ship.[5]

That change came from a sailor's comment because Mike Abrashoff had the wisdom to walk around asking questions and listening aggressively.

So leaders *learn* by walking around and asking questions, and then *teach* by helping people understand their role in the bigger picture.

Reading

If we are to set a good example for others, it's important to keep up with management trends and best practices. I believe that today's readers are tomorrow's leaders.

In four or five hours, you can learn about the life of a great person and the factors that contributed to his or her success. That knowledge gives you valuable insight as well as teaching points for helping other people learn from that person's experiences, achievements and mistakes.

I recommend many books to people. Here are the seven that I recommend most often:

1. *Built to Last: Successful Habits of Visionary Companies* by Jim Collins and Jerry I. Porras, 1994 and 1997, HarperCollins Publishers, Inc.

2. *The Leadership Engine: How Winning Companies Build Leaders at Every Level* by Noel M. Tichy and Eli Cohen, 2002, HarperCollins Publishers, Inc.

3. *Good to Great: Why Some Companies Make the Leap…and Others Don't* by Jim Collins, 2001, HarperCollins Publishers, Inc.

---

[5] D. Michael Abrashoff, *It's Your Ship: Management Techniques from the Best Damn Ship in the Navy*, Warner Books, New York, 2002, p. 47.

4. *The Richest Man in Babylon* by George S. Clason, 1988, Signet

5. *The Loyalty Effect: The Hidden Force Behind Growth, Profits, and Lasting Value* by Frederick F. Reichheld and Thomas Teal, 1996, Harvard Business School Press

6. *The E Myth Revisited: Why Most Small Businesses Don't Work and What to Do About It* by Michael E. Gerber, 1995 and 2001, HarperCollins Publishers, Inc.

7. *The Road Less Traveled: A New Psychology of Love, Traditional Values and Spiritual Growth* by Scott Peck, 1978, Simon & Schuster

I use *The Road Less Traveled* when I'm counseling advisors who are going through personal challenges. It's an interesting book, but I didn't "get it" until the third time I read it. The entire premise of the book is contained in the first three words: "Life is difficult."

If you understand that life is difficult, you have a chance to be happy, because every time something great happens to you, you'll say, "My goodness, I should be so thankful, because life is difficult, and look at this wonderful thing that happened to me."

And if you think that life is difficult and something ugly happens to you, you will say, "So what. C'est la vie." You don't blame anybody. You don't look up to the heavens and say, "Why me, Lord?" because you already know that life is difficult.

But if you think the opposite — that life is supposed to be a bowl of cherries — then every time something nice happens to you, you're going to say, "Well, I deserve it." And when something bad happens to you, you will blame everything and everyone around you.

Observing Other Successful People

We've all had great teachers. I watched Maury Stewart build the biggest agency in the world by having six meetings a week — every Monday through Saturday morning — with new agents about some aspect of the job (activity, results, marketing) or about integrity — doing the right thing when nobody's looking.

That had to be very tiring for him, but look at the impact it had. Maury was more than a great teacher. He was a mentor, and the difference between the two is significant: A mentor is a teacher who cares.

Using Situation Recognition

Wisdom is knowledge you accumulate over time that permits you to recognize a situation as something you should or should not proceed with. In both sales and management, we call this awareness "situation recognition."

Situation recognition first requires that you drill down and do what Jack Welch does — ask a lot of questions to find out what the issues are so you can help that person. Gather data.

Let's say I have an advisor who tells me that he consistently gets 12 referred leads a week and nine appointments a week, but at the end of a quarter, he has no sales. I know that situation. I recognize that something is wrong here. The first possibility is that the advisor is giving me erroneous data. The second is that he has a skill challenge — there are skills that he should have but doesn't, and we need to do some retrofitting with him. A third possibility is that this advisor is in the wrong market. For example, if he's prospecting people who can't pay credit card debt, that would explain why he's having a hard time closing sales.

Situation recognition is a skill you should teach to your advisors. We work hard with our advisors, getting them to listen to various scenarios and separating the relevant facts about an issue from the extraneous facts, just as lawyers are taught to separate the facts that are pertinent to the case from the "dicta," or extraneous details that are not relevant.

When we hire new advisors, it's impossible to teach them everything they'll need to know to be 100 percent proficient financial planners. But we can teach them situation recognition. For example, if an advisor's client has concerns about whether or not he'll be able to retire on time because of his financial situation, you recognize that situation as an accumulation challenge, and you can connect that advisor with someone in your organization who has expertise in where the client should be on the risk/reward curve.

Or your advisor's client might say, "My health is not that good, and I have some real concerns about my family should something happen to me." In this situation, you need someone who understands underwriting and understands what to do to provide peace of mind.

In our industry, some of the LUTC, CLU, ChFC and CFP courses provide good training for recognizing relevant facts when formulating financial plans for clients.

Leading Means Sharing

Many potential leaders don't understand the connection between leading and sharing.

People who have self-image problems have trouble being leaders, as do people in nonsharing environments, where the more *you* know, the more insecure *I* become. If you're working for me and I'm reluctant to teach you, it may be because I'm afraid you'll take my job someday. In that kind of environment, where people are not growing, leadership is seriously challenged.

But in many environments, especially in our industry, sharing is part of the culture. It is what Jim Benson, one of the authors of *22 Keys to Sales Success,* calls the *ingredients* of our business: collegiality and fraternity. In organizations where sharing is going on, leadership comes much more easily because people are conditioned to want to share the best practices that have worked for them.

> *Teachers affect eternity because they never know where their influence will stop.*
>
> MITCH ALBOM

You Take the Helm

- **Dedicate Your Life to Growing Others** — Allow the people around you to develop their leadership skills by transferring your knowledge to them. Remember, the more you give, the more you get. As Winston Churchill said, "We make a living by what we get; we make a life by what we give."

- **Ask Questions** — Walk around and ask your team members questions, and use these informal conversations as opportunities to teach them their role in achieving your organization's mission and vision. The Chinese say, "He who asks a question is a fool for five minutes; he who does not ask a question remains a fool forever."

- **Expand Your Knowledge Through Reading** — Keep ahead of the change curve by sharpening your mental faculties and your awareness of what's going on in the world. Today's readers are tomorrow's leaders.

- **Learn from the Success of Others** — Observe successful people in action and emulate their strategies.

- **Turn Your Experience into Wisdom** — Use situation recognition to read events and determine the best way to respond. Teach others to do the same.

- **Share Your Wisdom** — Avoid a zero-sum mindset, and be the living example of sharing wisdom. Foster an abundance mentality so people in your organization will want to share the best practices that have worked for them.

Chapter 7

Servant Leadership

Great Leaders Are Servants First

I BELIEVE 100 PERCENT in servant leadership. Robert Greenleaf began writing about this concept more than 40 years ago. His book *Servant Leadership*[1] is my primary resource on the subject, and I ask all new people coming into management in our organization to read it.

Greenleaf explains that his thoughts about servant leadership came together as he read Hermann Hesse's *Journey to the East*. Hesse tells a story about a band of men who are on a mythical journey. A servant named Leo accompanies the party; he not only does all the menial chores but also sustains the group with his spirit and song. When Leo disappears, the group falls into disarray, and the journey is abandoned. Years later, one of the men who had been on the journey finds Leo and discovers that he was the noble leader of the order that had sponsored the journey.

The message from Hesse's story, Greenleaf concluded, is that "The great leader is seen as servant first, and that simple fact is the

---

[1] Robert K. Greenleaf, *Servant Leadership: A Journey into the Nature of Legitimate Power and Greatness,* Paulist Press, Mahwah, New Jersey, 1977.

key to his greatness."[2] Greenleaf goes on to explain that, in Hesse's story, "Leadership was bestowed upon a man who was by nature a servant.... His servant nature was the real man, not bestowed, not assumed and not to be taken away. He was servant first."[3]

I view servant leadership as encompassing many elements, including a positive environment, trust, collaboration, compliments, communication and accountability. In a servant-leadership culture, these elements are visible every day as a regular part of doing business. If an element that is not congruent with servant leadership is introduced, the culture will spit it out like poison.

Picture a continuum: At one end is the true servant leader and at the other end is the autocrat. You can't have an autocratic person in the ranks of management in an organization that is devoted to servant leadership. It will cause far too many conflicts in terms of the way you manage the organization.

If I detect an autocratic attitude in somebody we're thinking about bringing into management, I will insist that that person read Greenleaf's book.

We lost one of our managers who had been with us for eight years. He simply wasn't a servant leader. His background and training were so dictatorial and one-sided that he found it very difficult to be a servant of the people who reported to him.

The office he managed was simply not a nice place to come to work. There was a "we/they" mentality. A rift existed not only among the advisors but also between the advisors and the administrative team members. The manager was never there when I came into the office. Because he was not a servant leader, he felt that he didn't have to be accountable. People who had problems had no one to go to because the servant leader was not there. The team members were very productive, effective and client-oriented, but they hated to come to work. That didn't happen in any other office in our system. In all our other offices, people loved to come to work.

---

[2]Greenleaf, p. 7.
[3]Greenleaf, p. 8.

It took eight years for the culture to spit this manager out because he had many great qualities, not the least of which was that he was a phenomenal leader in other ways. He was a tremendous leader, but he wasn't a servant leader. In a different culture, he might have succeeded.

Growing Management in Your Laboratory

Servant leaders are devoted to developing others. Think of your organization as a laboratory in which you try new things all the time so you can continue to infuse your organization with new concepts and ideas for growing people.

One way we grow people is to have all our advisors who qualify for Million Dollar Round Table (MDRT) "adopt" a new advisor and train him or her for six months to a year. At the end of that period, we pay the senior advisors. It's not a lot of money, but it recognizes the time and effort they've spent on developing a new person.

This process allows us to have all our new MDRT-level advisors try their hand at management. Because we hire so many young people straight out of college, we want them to have the opportunity to see if management appeals to them and if they excel at it.

If everyone tries managing, two things will happen. First, no one can look back and say, "I was discriminated against. I could have been a good supervisor or manager but was never given a chance." Everybody here gets a chance and is encouraged to try management. They may or may not like it. Second, when everyone tries managing, we have an opportunity to discover latent management talent that we might otherwise have missed.

Compliments Are Verbal Sunshine

I once read that a compliment is verbal sunshine. In a servant-leadership environment, there are many compliments. When people do something good, it's important to catch them at it, recognize it, remind them of it and tell other people about it. Servant leaders who are able to subordinate their own egos and their own need for recognition consistently look around and try to catch somebody in the act of doing something good for other people. The servant leader goes up to that person and reinforces the good behavior.

The more you reinforce good behavior, the higher will be the goals and performance levels of the people who receive those compliments. Servant leadership is about compliments, and it leads to people benefiting financially and having fun while they do it.

On a daily basis, advisors are subjected to a lot of rejection. They face constant frustration in trying to get their cases through underwriting; they deal with referred leads who refuse to see them and appointments who stand them up; and they have to contact 10 prospects to make three appointments…and then only one of them buys. So, two out of three times, advisors are rejected.

Because there's a lot of rejection in our world, it's vital that our offices be sanctuaries, places of refuge. That starts with the leader. A servant leader is in a position to create that kind of environment because he or she is constantly striving to make the office a pleasant place to work.

Dick McCloskey, the 2002 inductee into GAMA International's Management Hall of Fame, talks about the man who coached the southern California high school water polo team when Dick's boys were playing. This fellow had the longest winning streak of any coach in any sport in America. Dick studied him continuously and told me this story.

No matter how badly a young player messed up his performance, when he got out of the pool, the coach would walk over to him, put his arm around him and talk about the things the kid did right. He would tell the kid that he should feel good about them. Then he would say, "Now, the next time this thing happens, all you have to do is use some of the great attributes you have, and you'll get right over it."

Servant leaders build people up so they can succeed and aspire to higher levels.

We have a young woman here named Teresa Upchurch. I don't call her Teresa; I call her Smiley. Every morning when I walk in, I poke my head into her office if she's in there and say, "Hey, Smiley, how are you doing?" She'll say, "Hey, Mr. Phil." You know what that causes her to do? To keep smiling. She smiles more now than ever before. That's her brand, her trademark.

There are some universal truths, and one is that most people respond to legitimate compliments. I don't care if you're the president of a corporation, a board member or the person who sweeps the floors. We all like positive reinforcement. It's part of our genetic makeup.

If someone is caught in the act of doing something really great, it deserves notice in your firm or company publications and other venues. You can almost make a career out of finding people doing the right thing so you can reinforce that behavior.

Praise Publicly, Criticize Privately

People Are Fragile

People are fragile, and good field leaders understand that. For that reason, it's imperative that leaders criticize or address performance inadequacies privately. There are very few thick-skinned people. If everybody had thick skin, I could criticize publicly all I wanted. But I know better. I know that people hurt easily.

For me to chastise advisors in front of other people is not a welcome event in their day or my day, or in the day of almost anyone who's considered sane. Mentally healthy people don't like to be berated publicly. If I berate an advisor publicly, the first outcome will be some resistance on his part to me and my style. A grudge may form at that very moment. He also may have an avoidance reaction — he will want to avoid being in my presence in the future, because he doesn't want a recurrence of what just happened. Frightened people underperform.

The objective is not to soothe my own ego and place blame but rather to fix the problem, so I need to address the issue in private. If an advisor didn't see enough people last month, it's not appropriate or helpful for me to publicly berate him for failing. We need to fix the problem by having him make up for those numbers this month. I need to bring him in on an accountability basis to talk about why that happened and figure out tactics to keep it from recurring. The advisor will be in a receptive mood because he feels bad that he didn't perform up to expectations last month. He is not proud of that. If we talk about it, he's going to feel better because he'll be able to tell me what's been happening. Maybe his mother was ill and, for three of the four weeks of that performance period, he was at the hospital with her. Maybe his child was sick.

We are not *excusing* poor performance because (as you'll see in Chapter 21) that would be inconsistent with our high-performance, no-excuse culture. What we are doing is *addressing the issues* that caused the poor performance and identifying ways to resolve them so we can move forward.

"Praise in public, criticize in private" is a general rule in our organization, even in our Corporate Development Council (CDC) meetings. If someone is going to criticize someone else, it should be done on a one-on-one basis.

I Changed Companies Because of This Concept

In 1966, I was a 26-year-old assistant manager in the Philadelphia office of Hartford Life (formerly Columbia National). That year I received an award for ranking number one in sales nationally. In the company's White Plains office was a fellow named Bill Steinberg; he ranked number three.

Our respective managers made a $100 bet that year. (That was a lot of money then. I was making only $9,000 a year, so it was more than 1 percent of my income.) Each manager bet that his associate would win the number 1 slot for the coming year. My manager bet that I would beat Bill Steinberg, and Bill's manager bet that he would beat me.

The company invited the top 10 salespeople in the country to Hartford's home office, which was in Boston at that time, to visit with the senior officers. I'll never forget it. The 10 of us were sitting in the opulent boardroom at an ornate hand-carved conference table. The agency vice president (AVP) was at one end of the table and all the officers of the company were sitting in chairs up against the wall surrounding the table. The AVP looked over at Bill Steinberg, the number three guy in the country, and said, "Bill, why don't you tell everybody in the room what you're going to do in 1967 that you didn't do in 1966 that's going to allow you to be with us in 1968?"

He berated Bill Steinberg publicly in front of his nine peers and in front of everyone who was at all important in the company. I made up my mind at that very moment that I was leaving Hartford Life. Six months later, I was with Minnesota Mutual.

Coaching and Accountability

In a culture of servant leadership, team members know what's expected of them, and they know whether or not they are meeting those expectations.

In my role as a servant leader, one of the things I do religiously each month is to get a production report for all advisors. Those monthly production reports are very detailed and give me everything I need to know: the person's MDRT number, persistency, number of cases paid for, security and fee earnings, life commission and premium and income. Remember the saying, "If you can measure it, you can manage it."

The monthly report does two things. First, it helps me, as a manager, eliminate foxholes, which we talk about in Chapter 8. Second, it lets me measure people's progress. With 150 or more advisors in 10 states, it's not possible for me to see every one of them every quarter, let alone every month. So, to connect with them more personally, I send this monthly report to every advisor with a handwritten note. It might say, "Hi, Dan. I see you're on time for MDRT. Congratulations. You're just about on time for producing 100 cases this year. That would be a real feather in your cap. Good luck, Dan." That may be the only contact I am able to make with that advisor that month.

Personal touches are important. If your firm is to get scale and grow, you need to come up with ways to connect with your advisors so they know that the management team in their organization cares. You've probably heard the saying, "Often people care more about how much you care than about how much you *know*." When I review monthly reports, it's a way of saying that it's not about me; it's about the advisors who live in a world of rejection, and it's about my compensating for that rejection by giving them verbal sunshine, reaching out to them and acknowledging their worth, which I hope improves their self-image. People can't outperform their own self-image. Our job is to constantly help our advisors improve their self-image.

At North Star, we help people improve their sense of self-worth through our high-performance, no-excuse culture. We set high expectations for them and then help them meet their goals through accountability, encouragement and coaching.

To stay in our organization, advisors must qualify for Million Dollar Round Table beginning in their fifth year. If an advisor is not performing during his or her first four years, we go back to the basics. If an advisor's performance wasn't meeting our expectations, I would ask him into my office and say, "Tim, tell me about your goals and what's changed since January, when we sat down and agreed on them. What has happened since then?" Then we have to change one of two things. We either have to lower his goal or decide on a new activity level that will help him reach the goal. If you can measure it, you can manage it.

So we have to go back and measure what Tim did in the first six months of the year. If he had four new appointments per week in the first six months of the year, and he is only a quarter of the way toward his goal midway through the year, we know we need to double that activity and have eight appointments per week to get him to three-quarters of his goal.

This is a mathematical equation, not rocket science. If Tim wants to hit the goal, he'll need 12 new appointments a week in the last six months of the year to make up for the four that he had in the first six months. He must be willing to perform at the new level of activity; otherwise, we have to lower his goal.

Robert Greenleaf says that servant leaders make sure that other people's highest-priority needs are being served. The way we can test this, he says, is to ask ourselves if the people we serve are growing as people: "Do they, while being served, become healthier, wiser, freer, more autonomous, more likely themselves to become servants?"[4]

Let's make the answer to this question an enthusiastic "Yes!" as we strive to help people grow and prosper in our organizations.

> *Everyone can be great because anybody can serve. You don't have to have a college degree to serve. You don't have to make your subject and verb agree to serve. You only need a heart full of grace, a soul generated by love.*
>
> MARTIN LUTHER KING, JR.

---
[4]Greenleaf, pp. 13–14.

You Take the Helm

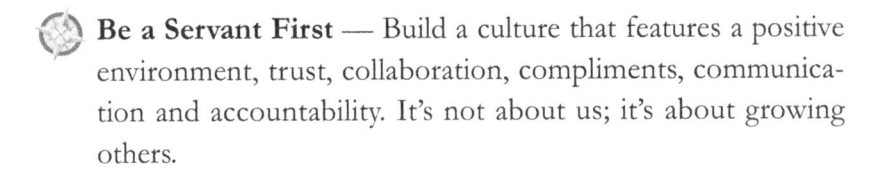

- **Be a Servant First** — Build a culture that features a positive environment, trust, collaboration, compliments, communication and accountability. It's not about us; it's about growing others.

- **Teach Others About Servant Leadership** — Educate all your team members to develop and reinforce your servant-leadership culture.

- **Be True to Your Culture** — In an organization that is devoted to servant leadership, you can't have an autocratic person in management. Try to recycle that person into a position that accommodates his or her disposition and skills.

- **Create Growth Opportunities** — Think of your organization as a laboratory in which you try many different ways to develop people. If advisors succeed in new and mysterious ways, learn from them.

- **Catch People Doing Things Right** — Compliment people on the things they do right. They will increase their performance and goals to meet your high regard for them. The best way to knock the chip off someone's shoulder is to pat him on the back.

- **Praise Publicly; Criticize Privately** — Help others become what they are capable of being. Address any performance issues in private. You'll get better results by throwing flower seeds on asphalt than you will by berating someone publicly.

- **Communicate Constantly** — A servant leader's job is to communicate with everyone as much as possible, both to help them gauge their progress and to let them know that you care about them as individuals.

- **Hold People Accountable to Their Goals** — People who are not performing up to par must do one of two things: increase their activity to achieve the goal or lower the goal.

- **Show That You Care** — Find ways to connect with your team members regularly so you can catch them doing something right, compliment them and help them improve their sense of self-worth, leading to a higher self-image.

Chapter 8

The Mars Group
Creating the Infrastructure for Your Success

I GOT A GREAT idea from *Built to Last*[1] that we now use at North Star. The authors say that every company should have a "Mars Group" composed of five to seven of the most credible and competent people who make that company what it is.

The way you determine who is in this group is to picture yourself ready to go to Mars in a spaceship. When you arrive, your mission will be to duplicate your existing company with no communication with anyone on Earth. You and this small group of people are going to start the company all over again and make it just as good as it was on Earth. Who would those people be?

I went through my company and looked at the people who were the highest paid, those who had the biggest titles and those who were considered to be the most important. I realized one of the people I *would* take on the Mars mission — Ed Deutschlander — was not in any of those categories.

---

[1] Jim Collins and Jerry I. Porras, *Built to Last: Successful Habits of Visionary Companies*, Harper-Collins Publishers, Inc., New York, 1997, p. 223.

On the basis of this exercise, I reorganized the company around the six people in my Mars Group. That was a big opportunity for Ed, because he was clearly doing an excellent job and was one of the key people in the company, but he was not being adequately compensated or recognized because of his youth and inexperience. Ed is now an executive vice president with North Star Resource Group and on track to lead it someday.

This exercise forces you to think, "Who's going to occupy those five to seven seats?" Remember what Jim Collins talks about in *Good to Great:* You've got to have the right people on the bus in the right seats.[2] These are the people who are going to drive the organization to the next level.

Today, my Mars Group is the think tank of our organization — the Corporate Development Council (CDC). This core group drives operational management at North Star and keeps us all accountable for our individual and collective results. It sets the pace for our success.

Every Friday at a box lunch meeting, the CDC convenes in my office to discuss where we are and where we need to go to. We look at our critical number, which I will explain momentarily. We look at who owns which of our tasks (only one person can own a task) and what the deadlines are. Anyone who is not here phones in for the meeting.

The Critical Number

Our Mars Group sets our goals and builds accountability into our structure at all levels of the organization. To ensure that we reach our goals, everyone in our organization has a critical number — one number — that tells us every day whether we're winning or losing. You don't wait until the end of the year to find out whether you won; you have to measure yourself in more frequent and focused terms.

---

[2] Jim Collins, *Good to Great: Why Some Companies Make the Leap... And Others Don't,* HarperCollins Publishing Inc., New York, 2001, p.13.

Our one critical number at North Star in 2006 was $550,000 of paid life commissions each month. We've found that when we focus on that life number, all other metrics work. Our securities, annuities, long-term care, disability income, fees, employee-benefits revenue and so on all reflect our success in achieving that goal.

Then we break that critical number down on a daily basis according to the number of working days in the month. A month may have 20, 21 or 22 working days. By dividing $550,000 by that number, we can look at our paid life commissions and know whether we've won or lost every day.

Every morning, Mars Group member Diane Yohn sends an email out to everyone in management, noting whether we won or lost the previous day. It's a green day if we make it, a red day if we don't. It's either red or green; there's nothing in between. No ties.

Each of our advisors has a critical number as well. Every new person's critical number is 30 forward appointments on the books. They may change that critical number after they begin producing at a certain level, but everybody starts with the number 30. Those 30 appointments could be over the next two weeks or the next six months. We don't care what the length of time is. We're simply saying that we want at least 30 appointments on every advisor's book at all times.

The reason we do that is because some people would have only six or seven appointments for the next week, but they'd say, "Don't worry about it. I've got a lot the following week." You have to be able to measure what you expect. The way we measure it is to require that all advisors have 30 appointments into the future — in ink, not pencil — on their books. During their first year, we ask advisors to bring their books with them into meetings, and we literally count the appointments. It's accountability. These meetings are held weekly for brand-new people as long as they're hitting our numbers. If they begin missing our numbers, we go to daily accountability via email. We call this "intensive care." They have to send their manager an email every morning stating what they plan to accomplish that day and an email every evening before they leave, reporting what they actually did accomplish that day.

Once our senior advisors have qualified for Million Dollar Round Table, they are on quarterly accountability. Every quarter, they have a review, which we discuss in Chapter 22.

Ownership

Whenever you have a task that needs to get done in an organization, there's a tendency for two or three people to volunteer to do it. That hasn't worked for us. A single person is responsible for each task or agenda item. That person may have a co-chair or five co-chairs, but there is only one chairperson. One person will either win or lose. Accountability and ownership rest with that one person.

Deadlines Are Critical

You have to set deadlines. A dream with a deadline is a goal, and a dream without a deadline is a fantasy. If you have a dream but you don't decide when you're going to make it happen, that's not a goal; it's a dream. In fact, it's daydreaming. When you put a deadline on it — "I will do this by next Thursday" — you've got a goal. It has a deadline, and you own it.

We require everyone at North Star to state their goals in writing. When new people come in, they don't fully understand the importance of writing down their goals. You see, once I write something down, it's no longer in my head. Once I write it down, I've put it into the public domain. Now if I miss that goal, it's not simply that I missed it in my own mind; I missed it in public. People accomplish more when they commit to their goals in writing and in a public venue.

We had a young man who was a Top of the Table producer in our Phoenix office. When we hired him, he was a 20-year-old graduate of the University of Arizona. He had to wait until his 21st birthday to get licensed, and he had only five months from the time he got licensed to qualify for the national convention. Nobody had ever done that. The convention qualification period was 15 months;

he had only five months and had never sold insurance or securities before. But he accomplished it because he had a goal.

That young man is the only person who has ever qualified for our national convention in five months. He not only had to write that business, he also had to pay for it, which is a difficult task because it sometimes takes two or three months for an underwriter to approve a case. But he did it in that short time because he had a goal — a dream with a deadline.

Set Bigger Goals

When I talk about the importance of goals and deadlines, it's because I've seen wonderful results in my own life, and I've seen the power that people experience when they set their sights on specific achievements.

When I was a senior in high school, I was the captain of my wrestling team. We had a sophomore on the team named Bill Kelly. I was a 138-pounder, and he was 133-pounder, and we went through our first 12 bouts together undefeated. We traveled down to Pottstown, Pennsylvania, to wrestle at Hill Preparatory School, which had won the national championship for three years in a row. The two wrestlers we were going to oppose were both national prep school champions. All four of us had 12–0 records.

Bill Kelly wrestled a fellow named Hiram Mercereau. Mercereau had been a three-time national prep school champion, had never been beaten in high school, and here he was wrestling against a little sophomore from Easton High School in Easton, Pennsylvania. At the end of the second period (out of three), Mercereau was beating Kelly 6–2 when he broke Kelly's arm. The little bone on Kelly's left elbow was just in there floating around.

Our wrestling coach, John Maitland, was also the high school biology teacher. He examined Kelly and found the broken bone; he took a towel, tied it into a knot, and threw it up into the air — the sign of surrender. Kelly jumped up and, with his good arm, grabbed the towel before it hit the mat, handed it back to Maitland, and said, "Coach, I'm going to beat this guy."

Maitland said, "Bill, you have a broken arm."

Bill was determined. "Coach, I'm going to beat him."

"Bill, you couldn't beat him with two good arms on your best day," the coach replied, "and you have a broken arm."

Bill repeated, "Coach, I'm going to beat him."

And he did! He went out with a broken arm and beat a three-time national prep school champion 7–6 in the third period. That was Mercereau's only loss in his entire four-year career — to a sophomore with a broken arm!

I wouldn't tell you that story if I didn't have the newspaper article to prove it. It was incredible. If Bill had wrestled that guy a thousand times, he would have lost all but that one day, which is the one day that he had a goal.

That was the moment when I realized the power of having a goal and the power of saying, "I will win." That's what Bill said: "I will win." He willed himself to win. That day changed my life. I realized that nothing is impossible.

We are capable of incredible achievements if we understand just how wonderful our minds are. In the early 1960s, a plastic surgeon named Maxwell Maltz wrote a book called *Psycho Cybernetics*. Maury Stewart was my general agent at that time, and he required all new agents to read that book. It shows that our success is limited only by how we limit ourselves.

People need to think bigger. They need to set the big, hairy, audacious goals that we talk about in Chapter 13 and not let other people rain on their parade or diminish their dreams.

One example of a person committing to big goals and achieving them is Shaun McDuffee, a senior partner in our Austin, Texas, office. When Shaun was 27 years old (he started when he was 21 in our Madison office but got his own unit at 27), he determined that he was going to build a $3 million commission unit in 10 years and he infected everybody with his goal. He put it into the public domain. He talked about it in every monthly bulletin with all his people. He did not hit $3 million in first-year collected life commissions in 10 years, but he did it in 11 years — because of the power of his goal. Most *agencies* never hit $3 million, but Shaun and his *unit* did.

Quarterly Deadlines Eliminate Foxholes

You may have heard the metaphor that some people crawl into a hole, pull the hole in after them and hide in it. They're in denial; they refuse to confront the brutal facts. I call these hiding places "foxholes." They jump into the foxhole to avoid the contest, the arena.

From a management point of view, we try to eliminate the foxholes. The solution we employ here is to set quarterly finish lines. This approach keeps people from waiting until November to try to qualify for MDRT. As you know, that's usually too late.

You only have to read the *Wall Street Journal* or your hometown newspaper to know that all publicly traded companies are measured on a quarterly basis. The Wall Street analysts say, "This is what you said you would earn over the past three months, and this is what you earned. On the basis of that, we're going to recommend that people buy your company's stock, hold the stock or sell it."

We believe that if a quarterly finish line is an effective tool for the CEO and board of directors of a publicly traded company, it can work just as well for an advisor and that's what we do. Here is an overview of our four quarterly finish lines.

First Quarter

We call our first quarter "March Madness." It's a takeoff on the U.S. college basketball tournament in which the top 64 teams compete for the championship. We got the idea for the contest in a GAMA study group from John Baier, a managing partner with New York Life. We take our top advisors and put them into brackets just as the NCAA does in college basketball.

Each week, based on their submitted life applications, advisors either advance or get beaten, and we bring it all the way down to March 31 (or whatever Friday is closest to March 31). That's the final week, and eight winners emerge from the sweet sixteen, four from the elite eight, two from the final four and finally one winner. We do that so that everybody is focused on that March 31 deadline. We have losers' brackets, and there are other prizes for people who do not win. We end up with 40 or 50 winners, and they're motivated right up to the March 31 deadline.

After our third year of running this contest, we increased the number of participants to the current level of 128 advisors instead of the original 64. Someday our goal is to run the contest with 256 advisors.

We've also tried to make it fairer. In the original contest, if two advisors in the same bracket did not score (both had zeros), they'd flip a coin to see who would advance. We didn't like having someone with a score of zero advance when a person in another bracket might have lost to someone else five to six but did not get to advance. Now we advance the person who had the most apps the previous week but lost out to a higher number, and we eliminate the two zero-producing advisors. You can't advance with a zero in our contest, just as you can't in life. The highest "loser" advances instead of either of two advisors with no submitted applications.

Second Quarter

Next, we decided to end our firm year on June 30 (instead of December 31, which is the end of the company year). Our awards to the Advisor of the Year, New Advisor of the Year, Disability Income Person of the Year, Securities Person of the Year, Long-Term Care Person of the Year and Annuity Person of the Year are all measured as of June 30. All our awards, plaques, prizes and bronzes are given to people in July at our summer convention in northern Wisconsin and are based on performance through June 30. That's our second checkpoint in the year.

Third Quarter

Our third-quarter finish line is called the Chairman's Challenge, in honor of Bob Senkler, chairman of the board of Securian and Minnesota Mutual. The top five people from this contest get to have dinner with Senkler. It is a great pleasure for Senkler, in spite of the fact that he pays for the winners' airfare and for the dinner.

We also have second and third tiers of prizes, along with $100 gift certificates for those who place 25th through 50th in the contest.

Last year, one of the five winners was Anthony Cameron, an ex-military guy in his late 20s. He was flown in for the dinner from Billings, Montana, and it was the biggest deal of his life. Anthony met his wife, who is from Billings, when they were both in the Air Force. He ended up going to work for his wife's father, who is one of our advisors. Now both Anthony and his father-in-law are advisors for us in Billings. From Anthony's military point of view, it was like having dinner with the President of the United States. He was so excited, and I sat him right next to Senkler. This kid was in seventh heaven. It was the first thing that he's won since he's come on board as an advisor. It was a great, great experience for him. His father-in-law has been with Securian for 20 years, and *he's* never had dinner with Bob Senkler.

Fourth Quarter
In the fourth quarter, we focus on Million Dollar Round Table qualification, which ends December 31, along with all the Securian company clubs and conventions.

We've eliminated the foxholes. We've eliminated the places to hide: every quarter is the last quarter. People can't procrastinate and say, "Oh, I'll make it up in the last quarter." It's always the last quarter.

This great management technique has contributed immensely to North Star's productivity and success.

> *The reason most people never reach their goals is that they don't define them, or ever seriously consider them as believable or achievable. Winners can tell you where they are going, what they plan to do along the way and who will be sharing the adventure with them.*
>
> DENIS WATLEY

You Take the Helm

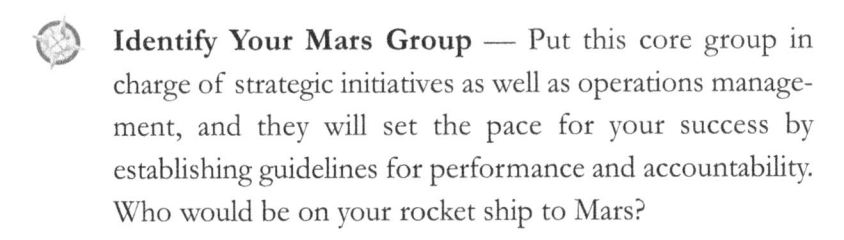

- **Identify Your Mars Group** — Put this core group in charge of strategic initiatives as well as operations management, and they will set the pace for your success by establishing guidelines for performance and accountability. Who would be on your rocket ship to Mars?

- **Set Your Firm's Critical Number** — Know every day whether you're winning or losing.

- **Set a Critical Number for Advisors** — Allow them to change that number only after they begin producing at your minimum success level.

- **Assign Ownership to One Person** — Many people will work on the task, but only one person will win or lose.

- **Set Deadlines** — A dream with a deadline is a goal. A dream without a deadline is a fantasy. A pattern of fantasies becomes a nightmare of turnover and failure.

- **Put Your Goals in the Public Domain** — People accomplish more when they commit to their goals in writing, in a venue where other people will see them.

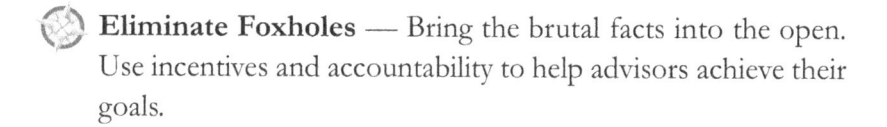

- **Set Grand Goals** — Our success is limited only by the limits we place on ourselves. We are capable of amazing achievements if we understand just how incredible our potential is.

- **Eliminate Foxholes** — Bring the brutal facts into the open. Use incentives and accountability to help advisors achieve their goals.

Chapter 9

Focus on Relationships

THE SINGULAR skill that most advisors possess that allows them to succeed in our great business is their ability to form relationships with clients by earning their trust. While other characteristics are important and necessary, face-to-face people skills are clearly paramount in our business.

For that reason, our advisors need not worry about having their positions outsourced to other countries, as is happening with many jobs in America today, or about being replaced by a computer.

Advisors' People Skills Protect Their Jobs
At LAMP 1996, Thomas P. Burns made a general session presentation titled "Redefining Our Role as Leaders in a High-Risk Culture." In that discussion, he said that we are all feeling more pressure to work even harder than we have in the past because of global competition and the Internet.

Globalization of the Economy
The globalization of our economy is a huge source of stress for many people, not only because many jobs are being outsourced to

other countries, but also because of the pressure that this international labor competition has placed on benefits, earnings and job-performance expectations.

In his 2006 book *The World Is Flat*, Tom Friedman describes how globalization and exponential advances in digital technology have made it possible to do business instantaneously with billions of other people across the planet. Innovative start-ups all over the world drive this globalization, especially in India and China, where people can compete for — and obtain — low-wage manufacturing and information jobs as well as highly skilled research and design work.[1]

A much-quoted 2003 study by Goldman Sachs said: "… India's economy … could be larger than Japan's by 2032, and China's larger than the US by 2041 (and larger than everyone else as early as 2016)."[2]

Many employers might prefer to be paternalistic organizations that take care of their employees, but they no longer have that luxury. Those who do so proceed at their own peril. We're seeing a marked decline of defined-benefit pension plans, an increasing shift of health care costs to employees and higher productivity expectations and requirements. These are just a few of the manifestations of the accelerating phenomenon of outsourcing, caused by globalization.

You know that our economy is suffering when General Motors has to renegotiate its defined-benefit pension plans and lay off 30,000 workers to save the company. For each car that comes off the line, $1,500 in costs goes toward major medical insurance for GM's workers.[3] In Japan, they don't have those issues, and in Europe they have those issues to a far lesser extent. Clearly, that puts American companies at a disadvantage. Americans are not only competing with

---

[1] Thomas L. Friedman, *The World Is Flat: A Brief History of the Twenty-First Century*, Farrar Straus Giroux, New York, 2006.
[2] Dominic Wilson and Roopa Purushothaman, Goldman Sachs, Economics Paper No. 99, Oct. 1, 2003, p. 3.
[3] Ceci Connolly, "U.S. Firms Losing Health Care Battle, GM Chairman Says," *The Washington Post*, Feb. 11, 2005, p. E-1.

other Americans but also with billions of other hard-working, less well-paid people around the world.

But I confidently submit to you that our advisors need not fear that their positions will be outsourced. While X-rays and tax returns are being read in India, our advisors' jobs remain secure because our advisors are in the relationship and trust business. Securing a client's trust requires a face-to-face initial interview, and building a relationship requires face-to-face follow-up. This contact cannot be accomplished from halfway around the world.

Life insurance must be first understood and then explained by committed people who own it themselves, believe in the character required to buy it and can persuasively describe its advantages — in person. That's tough to outsource.

The Internet

It's true that some people buy commodities on the Internet. They buy some of our products based on price, not based on an overall plan. There will always be do-it-yourself insurance and financial services consumers, much like homeowners who buy their own tools and supplies at home-improvement stores. These people are missing out on the benefit of having access to the expertise and experience of our advisors — the people of integrity we hired out of college. What they are getting is information, not wisdom. Computers don't dispense wisdom.

All computers should come with warning labels that say, "Wisdom not included. Use at your own risk." Wisdom comes from human experience, and even the best Web site cannot begin to compare with the advice that a well-trained, educated, knowledgeable and compassionate advisor can provide to a client.

Keeping the Planes in the Air

As field leaders, we need to remind our advisors about two important points regarding computers.

1. They can use technology to enhance their professionalism, but they should resist the temptation to let computer time cut into the time they personally spend helping clients or trying to get in front of future clients.
2. They need not be concerned about being replaced by computers as long as they focus on face-to-face distribution and delegate the computing to others.

Spending excessive time with computers has cost more than a few new advisors their careers. This is a real temptation today, given the many conveniences that technology offers. Computers and their inherent conveniences are merely accelerators — they help us get information more quickly. As a result, all of us, our advisors included, are prone to "analysis paralysis" — the irresistible temptation to spend hours in front of the computer analyzing our competition, our potential clientele, the numbers and everything else.

Field leaders should focus on ways to convince advisors that they would be well advised to spend time in front of people and leave the computer work to others who have different skills and responsibilities. After all, the majority of our advisors are attracted to this business because they love people and want to help them. Instead, too many of them spend hours at the keyboard preparing logical arguments for a sale, even though they know from their training and experience that the client's ultimate decision to do business with them will be largely an emotional one based on trust, not on numbers.

So how do we get our advisors to resist the temptation to become keyboard junkies? My experience has shown that we won't have much influence over veteran advisors. Experience has also taught us that the more successful our advisors are, the less ability we will have to modify their behavior. This is easy to accept as long as we keep in mind that they are, after all, our customers.

We have far more impact on our newer advisors, who follow a regimented training program in their first 90 days on the job. During that time, we as managers must help our advisors focus on expanding the time they invest in relationships and not on those tasks that can be done easily by others. We constantly coach our advisors that, "If you do $20-an-hour work, that's what you'll be paid. If you want $400 an hour, then spend the greater part of your time with clients and prospects."

Administrative and marketing assistants play a vital role in keeping our advisors in front of clients.

MDRT research has shown that Top of the Table qualifiers spend more time with clients than Court of the Table (COT) qualifiers, and COT qualifiers spend more time with clients than MDRT qualifiers. So there is clearly a direct link between increasing face-to-face time with clients and increasing productivity.

Learn from Southwest Airlines' Success

Keeping advisors in face-to-face meetings with prospects and clients is analogous to Southwest Airlines' extremely successful ability to "keep the planes in the air."

In 1996, *Harvard Business Review* published an article about how Southwest Airlines is able to keep its planes flying longer hours than its rivals and to provide frequent departures with fewer aircraft.[4]

Southwest's strategy was to schedule flights based on 15-minute turnarounds at the gate. The company eliminated first-class seating, meals, seat assignments, baggage transfers and travel agents. And they fly and service only one type of aircraft.[5]

By 2005, Southwest Airlines had been profitable every year for 31 years, an unsurpassed record in the highly turbulent and frequently unprofitable airline industry. During the same period, most of Southwest's competitors struggled to achieve even three or four consecutive years of profitability. Southwest also ranked high in employee satisfaction and retention.[6]

---

[4]Michael E. Porter, "What Is Strategy?" *Harvard Business Review*, November–December 1996, p. 64.
[5]Porter, p. 64.
[6]Jody Hoffer Gittell, *The Southwest Airlines Way*, McGraw-Hill, New York, 2005, p. 3.

In short, Southwest Airlines accomplished this remarkable track record by keeping the planes in the air.

The Southwest Airlines case study provides the perfect metaphor to use when teaching assistant team members what their job is. They learn that advisors make money only when they are in front of people — when the planes are in the air. Their job description therefore begins and ends with that mandate. Their performance and task orientation must be measured with the yardstick of this single question: "Will this keep the advisor in front of people?" If the answer is yes, then the assistant should schedule the advisor to proceed with that task. If the answer is no, then the assistant will perform the task for the advisor.

The assistant makes appointments and schedules client reviews so that the advisor can be in front of people as much as possible. The assistant also performs related tasks, such as following through on attending-physician requests and policy-service requests, making beneficiary and address changes, preparing proposals, making competitive comparisons, scheduling licensing and continuing education requirements, monitoring everything for regulatory compliance and so on. These are all important and necessary tasks, but they "ground" our advisors. We have learned that we can achieve success more easily by teaching the *assistant* new strategies than we can by trying to change the behavior of a successful *advisor*. One is a team member, while the other is our customer.

Coach your advisors to measure their assistants' performance by this benchmark, and everyone will benefit.

I made a similar presentation recently to a group of Farm Bureau field leaders in Des Moines, Iowa. Afterward, I received several emails thanking me for making the point that the role of administrative assistants is to keep advisors in front of clients. Attendees at that meeting told me in person and emails, "Thanks — we've never been able to convince people what the benchmark is, which is that administrative and marketing assistants should keep the planes in the air, or keep advisors in front of clients. You made it so clear — if administrative assistants do something to keep advisors in front of people, they are doing their job. If they do things that keep advisors from being in front of people, they are failing at their job."

That is the benchmark.

> *When dealing with people, remember you are not dealing with creatures of logic, but creatures of emotion.*
> DALE CARNEGIE

You Take the Helm

- **Stress the Value of Relationship-Building Skills** — Reassure your advisors that they need not worry about their positions being outsourced to other countries or replaced by technology. Their face-to-face relationship-building skills protect their valuable careers.

- **Focus on Relationships** — Where relationships are concerned, teach your advisors to follow the words of Andrew Carnegie: "Put all your eggs in one basket, and watch that basket." Face-to-face time beats computer time every time.

- **Keep the Planes in the Air** — Coach your advisors to ensure that their administrative and marketing assistants perform the duties that will make it possible for them to invest more of their time with clients.

Chapter 10

The Flywheel

Life Insurance Puts Client Relationships in Motion

A FLYWHEEL is a heavy device that captures, stores and transfers energy and momentum to an engine. It takes great strength and many consecutive pushes to get a flywheel moving, but then the flywheel begins to gain momentum, turning faster and faster — so forcefully that it's almost unstoppable.

In our industry, life insurance is the flywheel that captures, stores and transfers energy and momentum in client relationships. In other words, when you focus on life insurance as your core offering to clients, it sets the stage for your advisors to provide additional products.

The Slippery Slope

It's very hard to sell life insurance and very easy to sell mutual funds, so advisors often gravitate toward selling securities at the expense of their life insurance sales. I call this temptation the "slippery slope." The slippery slope represents any decision that an advisor makes to choose a path of convenience or greed over a path of integrity. Here are some examples of the slippery slope:

When Advisors Choose This Path	Instead of This One
Order Taker	Life Insurance Advisor
Broker	Financial Planner
Gatherer	Hunter
Asset Accumulator	Trusted Advisor
Commodity	Relationship
Coasting	Purpose
Income	Integrity

In my 44 years in this industry, I have yet to see a good stockbroker become a good life insurance salesperson, but I have seen many life insurance people become successful stockbrokers. To go from selling life products to selling mutual funds is to go from hard to easy. Almost anyone can sell stocks. But the reverse — transitioning from the easy sale to the hard — is almost impossible.

John McTigue, a leading managing partner with Northwestern Mutual in Chicago, addressed this subject in his LAMP 2006 general session presentation. John said that a financial plan without life insurance was like playing the lottery. He said that if you are aware of advisors' temptation to sell securities at the expense of life insurance sales, you should set up the metrics in your firm or agency to adjust for that. At North Star, we do this by emphasizing our critical number, which is currently $550,000 of paid life commissions per month (see Chapter 8 for details).

Life Insurance Allows Advisors to Build Client Relationships

Life insurance is the dramatic explosion of money that materializes at precisely the moment it's needed, enabling kids to stay in their neighborhood schools, playgrounds and churches when a parent dies. It removes the need for surviving spouses to become part-time parents when their children need them most. It saves jobs and keeps businesses from failing when a partner or key employee dies. This happens because an advisor made the critical presentation of facts and because an insured person with character heeded that advice. If the insured breadwinner in a family dies, the spouse will have peace of mind knowing that the death benefit will be delivered just when it is most needed.

The life insurance focus is the flywheel that builds client relationships. The sale of life insurance requires advisors to get on a personal level with a client — talking about obligations, family, love of others — and enables advisors to develop a relationship of trust. The client learns to trust the advisor because he or she has been an advocate (to borrow Dr. Csaba Sziklai's phrase[1]) for those who have no voice — the children and spouse, who would suffer significant financial distress should the client die. The person who initiated that difficult conversation about protecting loved ones naturally ascends to a position of trust with the client.

Once trust is established, the client will feel comfortable with that advisor and will prefer to conduct transactions for other products — such as long-term care, disability income, mutual funds, IRAs or 401(k)s — exclusively with the advisor.

A beautiful enigma in our industry is that the more your life insurance sales go up, the more your mutual fund sales go up. But the opposite is not so. A firm or agency can have mutual fund sales exceeding $20 million of gross dealer concessions, but it does not follow that its life insurance sales will go up.

Life insurance continues to be the most powerful product we can provide to clients. If you continue to use life insurance as your metric, and you continue to put your shoulder to that flywheel, additional business will follow. And if your advisors understand this phenomenon, not only will they be less tempted to slide down the slippery slope, but their production will increase, their service to humanity will improve and their client relationships will be strengthened and solidified.

---

[1] Dr. Csaba Sziklai is a Hungarian-born clinical psychologist who spent 30 years coaching and studying insurance professionals and the insurance sales process, then went on to develop the "Advocacy System™" for insurance sales training and recruiting. His consulting practice is based in Park City, Utah.

> *If you are willing to only do what is easy, life will be hard. But if you are willing to do what's hard, life will be easy.*
>
> T. Harv Eker

You Take the Helm

- **Be Strong Enough in Character to Make the Hard Sale First** — The life insurance focus enables advisors to build relationships and earn a position of trust with clients.

- **Use Life Insurance as Your Metric** — The miracle of life insurance is the flywheel that facilitates the sale of all of your other products.

- **Repeat the Message** — What differentiates your advisors from stockbrokers is the religion of life insurance and its rightful place in any sound financial plan. Never miss an opportunity to teach this critical lesson to your advisors. Repeat, repeat, repeat.

Author's Note

I'd like to share what I believe is a little-known strategy that can help your advisors provide even more value to their clients who buy life insurance. It's called "the cost of waiting." I came into the insurance business relying on this concept and, because of it, succeeded in convincing many clients to take action rather than procrastinate.

In a recent set of quarterly reviews, I was startled to find out that seven new advisors in a row whom I met with had never heard of this concept! I later asked Diane Yohn, vice president of client services on our Corporate Development Council, to check into this. What we learned was that something had slipped between the cracks in our training program. Here was one of the best tools that I had learned as a new agent, and we at North Star had stopped teaching it. You can bet that the situation has been corrected.

This is wonderful news for our clients, and it demonstrates the value that we can provide for them.

The following chart illustrates the cost of waiting to purchase life insurance. While the dollar amounts will change for different products, the end results are the same.

The Cost of Waiting
($100,000 Whole-Life Policy for a Male)

Policyholder's Age	Annual Cost Of Premium	Cash Paid Into Policy At Age 65	Cash Value Of Policy At Age 65
36	$1,334	$40,020	$89,600
37	$1,386	$40,128	$86,200
38	$1,441	$40,219	$82,800
39	$1,499	$41,385	$79,600
40	$1,560	$41,449	$76,400
41	$1,624	$41,582	$73,200

You'll see from the chart that the annual premium cost goes up slightly every year. But the cash value of the policy actually decreases. Here's why. (This is generic and not company-specific).

Regardless of when a person begins paying into the contract — age 35 or age 40 — the premium will be approximately $40,000. But, through the miracle of compound interest, the cash value that he will have at age 65 changes dramatically. For example, the cash value for somebody who starts at 35 is $89,600. Starting at 36 brings it down to $86,200, $3,400 less. The cost of waiting to buy this whole-life policy is more than $3,000 a year, and the client has one less year of coverage.

Most advisors use their prospects' or clients' birth dates to trigger a buying opportunity. We don't use their birth date; we use their insurance birth date, which is usually six months past their birth date because most companies use "age nearest birthday" when pricing a policy. For example, my birth date is October 18. Therefore, on April 18, I become one year older for insurance purposes because I'm closer to 66 than I am to 65 on that day.

Here's what we were trained to do in Maury Stewart's agency. Anywhere from 10 to 30 days before a client's insurance birth date, we would call and say, "I know that you're thinking about the plans that we reviewed last year. I've got to bring to your attention the fact that in 10 days, you will become closer to your next birthday, and that can cost you as much as $3,000 if you wait till then. If you're thinking about going with that plan, please consider doing it on or before April 17th and not after April 17th." A great sense of urgency is justifiably applied using this sales concept.

Communicating this information provides a significant benefit to the client. The premium is lower the younger the policyholder is. The client also benefits from the increased cash value of the policy. While the commission for the advisor is less when the client purchases at an earlier age, the benefit to the advisor and firm is that the cost differential may help a procrastinating client to take action.

Why would a manager want to know this concept? Because it can be a very powerful teaching tool in your firm. The concept presents an opportunity to teach advisors the value of following up with their clients and prospects and helping them understand yet another cost of their procrastination. And for a manager, it's also another opportunity to be a honeybee.

Chapter 11

People Love Specialists

SPECIALIZING IN particular markets serves many purposes. First and foremost, it is a client-centered strategy, so your clients' needs are best served under this type of arrangement.

Second, specialization allows you to differentiate yourself from your competitors and to be much more selective. You're not interested in talking to just anybody. You're only interested in talking to people in your "profile market" because that's where you spend all of your time, learning and energy.

Third, specialization reinforces your sales. Being very specific makes clients realize that you understand their unique problems. They don't have to spend their time educating you about the intricacies of their business. You already know about them.

Finally, referrals come more easily when you specialize. For example, pharmacists know scores of other pharmacists, so they can refer you to their colleagues, enabling you to become further involved in that market. The more pharmacists you work with, the more each one benefits, because your learning curve decreases and your knowledge about that market increases.

Why We Began Specializing

Forty years ago, almost every case sold was in competition, and you had to figure out a way to differentiate yourself. Quick, package-type selling was not very effective in the professional markets, so we developed a system that built relationships and trust. In the affluent marketplace, people are interested in two things: (1) Can I trust you? and (2) Are you competent?

Let's take the second question first: Are we competent? At North Star, our strategy is to recruit advisors to specialize in professional markets — physicians, dentists, veterinarians, pharmacists, engineers and owners of small to medium-sized businesses. These professionals are very bright (they wouldn't be able to get into those schools if they weren't), which aligns perfectly with our strategy of hiring business graduates from four-year accredited colleges who are in the top quarter of their class. They, too, are very bright, and the field of financial planning is a natural extension of the subjects they've been studying in college.

Now let's look at the first question that concerns our clients — can they trust us? That is a hard thing to be able to determine in one or even two interviews. As the number of interviews increases, the prospect's comfort level begins to rise; thus, the evolution of our five-part client-interview process.

The Five-Part Client-Interview Process

We bring our affluent clients, who are also specialists, together with our highly educated advisors in a structured five-part interview process.

A new advisor's first 20 client appointments are always conducted with an experienced MDRT-level trainer. One reason for this process is market conduct and compliance. We want to make sure somebody else is in on the interviews when a new advisor gets his or her first 20 clients. If we lose the new advisor, the clients are not left high and dry — someone who is familiar with them and their situation will pick up the service work. A by-product of this requirement is better firm persistency.

The second reason for including an MDRT-level trainer in the first interview is that we want to make sure the client is not misinformed by a new advisor who may not yet have all the pertinent facts and information.

Third, as a client-centric organization, we want to ensure the high quality of the advice we give. The wisdom and experience of a senior advisor contribute to that end.

Following is an overview of the five-part interview process. We call the meetings 1, 2, 3-A, 3-B and 4.

Interview 1 — Introduction
During the first appointment, our advisors explain what North Star does and how we're compensated.

Interview 2 — Financial Planning Education
The focus of the second interview is education. We begin, in a generic way, to explain why people need financial goals as well as other kinds of goals in life. Then we describe some of the tools we use to help people achieve their financial goals.

Interview 3-A — Product Education; Fact and Data Gathering
During this interview, the advisors find out where clients stand and determine their needs and wants.

The advisors discuss what products the client should implement and the asset-accumulation products they should have; for example, money-market funds or mutual funds. This might be the first time they've ever put money in the stock market. Remember, these are brand-new professionals, such as new resident physicians.

By now, the relationship is so good that the advisors are comfortable reminding clients to bring their checkbook with them for the next appointment, which is the implementation interview. (All appointments other than those with business owners take place in our offices. Physicians stopped making house calls a half-century ago, and we followed that model soon after.)

Interview 3-B — Implementation; Request for Referrals

Nothing is actually sold until the fourth meeting. By the time the client and his or her spouse get to this interview, where all implementation takes place, a strong bond has been formed between the individual or couple and the advisor.

During this interview, the advisor makes recommendations, on the basis of the information and data that have been collected, about which products the client should use.

Our advisors also ask for referred leads during this interview. The key is to remind the clients that we specialize in their professional area. Our advisors are taught to give names rather than ask for them. That is, the advisor uses a source such as a company directory, signage in a lobby, or the Internet to compile a list of professionals, then shows this list to the client and asks if there is any reason why these people should not be called on. This approach is more effective than asking for names. We teach our advisors to ask whether the client has any objection to being used as a reference if one of the people on the list has questions about the type of work we do or our reliability.

Interview 4 — Contract Signing

In the final interview, the advisors put it all together. By this time, they have obtained approvals from insurance companies for products and any securities are delivered. This is when the exchange of the actual fee plan (if included) and the products takes place, and the contracts are signed.

The services that we provide are sometimes a function of the relationship and the sale that's taking place, and sometimes provided on the basis of fees. In our situation, clients have an option to choose a fee-only approach or to take a commission-only approach. In many cases, they take both. In other words, they'll have a plan drawn for a fee and will rely on the planner to execute the recommendations that are in the plan.

This is an important point. Some advisors are timid about being compensated by both commissions and fees. But, for example, an internist who examines you and recommends surgery does not eliminate his or her fee just because someone else (the surgeon) will charge you for executing the plan. Think of the fee as a "proof of commitment" from the prospect.

About Attorneys

Over the past 40 years, we have had many false starts with our young advisors trying to get into the attorney market; in fact, that market has proved to be a career-ender for many people who come into our business.

In law school, students learn a great deal about many, many subjects. (My own one year of law school gave me just enough knowledge to make me dangerous!) Many lawyers believe they know more about insurance contracts than our advisors do. They tend to absorb a lot of an advisor's information, then commoditize our recommendations and either buy products on the Internet or put them up for bids, rather than forming a relationship with the advisor, as many other professionals do.

In our entire system and in all my experience, there is only one exception to this general scenario. We have an advisor in Madison, Wisconsin, Thomas A. Haunty, who specializes in working with lawyers. Tom has written approximately 60 articles for the *American Bar Association Journal* and was approached by the ABA Foundation to teach financial planning to young lawyers in the Chicago area. (See the Author's Note at the end of this chapter for details about how Tom has excelled in this difficult market.)

That's the exact place a young advisor wants to be — recognized as a person who adds value to the market and is an expert in his or her area. Specialization allows this to happen.

> *Gather in your resources, rally all your faculties, marshal all your energies, focus all your capacities upon mastery of at least one field of endeavour.*
>
> JOHN HAGGAI

You Take the Helm

- **Specialize for the Client's Benefit** — Clients are best served by advisors who understand the nuances of their specific professional markets.

- **Specialize for Your Firm's Benefit** — Differentiate yourself in the marketplace, reinforce your sales and obtain high-quality referred leads.

- **Build a System that Builds Relationships** — Take your clients through a structured process that answers two critical questions: Are you competent? Can I trust you?

Author's Note

The following narrative describes how Thomas A. Haunty has gained a foothold in the attorney market.

Since 1982, I have worked with lawyers who represent my estate-planning clients. During that time, those lawyers have been key centers of influence from whom I have sought referrals.

From the beginning, I noticed a large disconnect, and I knew I could resolve it: Attorneys know a lot about money — they spend a lot of time protecting money, going after it and litigating over it. But few of them understand how to manage their own money or how to do for themselves what they so vigilantly advocate for their clients. It's like the cobblers' kids going without shoes.

A lot of lawyers feel very bad about their lack of knowledge, and I play on that in a nice way, explaining that I can solve this dilemma for them. I present myself as the most vigilant advocate they'll ever meet to represent them in getting the most out of their money.

To reach attorneys in my area, I suggested to the editor of the Dane County Bar Association newsletter that I write a column about lawyer finances. I wrote one almost every month from 1987 through 1993 (pre-compliance days).

In 1993, I expanded my outreach by approaching the editors of the *ABA Journal,* the largest-circulation magazine for lawyers in the United States. They had a finance column, but — as I gently but firmly pointed out to them — the information they were giving out was generic. I told them that the best magazine for lawyers in the country was missing an opportunity to address lawyers' specific money issues. The editor, Steve Keeva, looked around the United States at several advisors who worked with lawyers and selected me to write articles for lawyers about their finances.

Since 1993, I've written about 60 articles on lawyer finances for the *ABA Journal* and have been extensively quoted. Having their blessing on my credibility is a huge indirect endorsement. I've also written articles that have been published in *Kiplinger's Personal Finance, Wisconsin State Journal, Capital Times, Middleton Times Tribune* and other newspapers and magazines over the years — probably 100 articles altogether. These articles have opened up numerous opportunities for me to get referrals to prospective lawyer clients.

I've made presentations to the Chicago, Texas and Portland Bar associations. I've spoken at the third-largest law firm in the world — DLA Piper Rudnick Gray Cary — via a simulcast seminar to all their young lawyer groups across the country. Additionally, I've spoken since 2004 at each of the biannual Young Lawyers Division conventions. This opportunity came about through the marketing efforts of the American Bar Endowment (ABE), the nonprofit arm of the ABA, for which I serve as volunteer financial advisor.

One day a month I have a "call-in day." Young lawyers can sign up to speak with me, free of charge, for 10 to 15 minutes to address any financial issue. This puts me in touch with 20 to 25 lawyers from all over the country every month, and I'm able to follow up with them. I can promote disability income coverage, life insurance and other sound planning strategies for these young lawyers early in their careers.

With the assistance and guidance of Todd Bramson, I've just published my first book, *Real-Life Financial Planning for the Young Lawyer*.

I call my work with lawyers my "practice subspecialty" because they are not my only clients, but also because they refer me to many other interesting cases. I manage settlement assets from lawsuits and place life insurance in their clients' estate plans. Also, lawyers often quit law and go on to do other things, such as starting businesses or running nonprofits. I handle the benefits for those organizations, pension rollovers and so on.

At this point, I believe I can go out and get as many lawyer clients and law firms as I want, because I have the credibility, experience and specific expertise that very few advisors have (or want to have).

In fact, I run my practice like a law practice — I use "case" terminology and carry myself like a lawyer. I like being detailed, dressing formally for work and being the expert.

I like working with lawyers because I find them to be straightforward. They tell it like it is. Unlike physicians, for example, who often think they know everything because they save lives all day, lawyers will tell you what they do and do not know. On the other hand, lawyers are difficult to work with because they are skeptical about everything. You have to work through their tough outer skin, get them to relax and remind them that they are their own most important client and they need to take care of themselves.

Two reasons I've been successful working with lawyers is that I am persistent and I've worked hard to forge a target niche. John Savage once told me, "All you have to do is last," and he was right. Too many agents and advisors quit right before they could have been successful. In my opinion, anybody can sell to a doctor, and every advisor is going after them. So I thought, why not skip the competition and go where there is an unfulfilled need? This approach has paid off — I currently manage more than $135 million in assets.

The fact that I've been doing this for 24 years is a source of comfort for my prospects — they know that I'm not learning about their profession on their time. Because I have North Star's culture and values behind me, and because I am trustworthy, I know that I can make a big difference in my clients' lives.

Chapter 12

Blended, Not Balanced

NOT ONLY IN OUR industry but throughout the world, people talk about how their lives are a delicate balancing act. This concept reminds me of a story about the high-wire aerialist, the Great Zumbrati.

Zumbrati had just finished walking a tightrope across Niagara Falls on a very windy day, and he was glad it was over. He was met at the end by an enthusiastic supporter with a wheelbarrow. After the man lavishly praised Zumbrati, he asked him to recross the tightrope using the wheelbarrow instead of the pole. Zumbrati declined, declaring that it was far too windy. The man persisted. Finally, Zumbrati said, "You really believe in me, don't you?" The man said that he did indeed.

"Fine, then," Zumbrati said, "Get in the wheelbarrow."

When your primary concern in life is *balance*, as it was for Zumbrati, an outside force (in his case, the wind) can throw you off. If you *blend* the various elements of your life instead, you are less likely to be thrown off course by the adverse circumstances that will sometimes occur.

We should coach people to realize that the various aspects of their lives are not in opposition to one another. The secret is to blend all these components: spirituality, home life, community involvement, health and career. You do not have to balance one aspect of your life against another; rather, you can blend them into a whole. In his book *Working Without a Net*, Morrie Shechtman says, "Who we are personally is inextricably connected to who we are professionally; the goal is to lead *blended*, not *balanced*, lives."[1]

Let's assume that you had a terrible day at the office. It would take a pretty special person to leave that at the office and not take it home. In fact, I don't believe that we're hardwired that way. If you're really devastated — if, for instance, you've just been fired — it would be impossible for you not to take that home. People who promote the concept of *balance* would say, "Hey, why don't you just leave that at the office and go home and be the best spouse and parent you can be?" Forget about it. It sounds good, but believe me, you'll have trouble with the execution.

By the same token, if a woman has a serious argument with her spouse at home about the right way to raise their children, then leaves in a huff for the office, it is unrealistic to think that she's going to get to work and be as perfect as usual. It's a fact of life that serious frustrations in your office life will carry over to your home life, and vice versa.

The trick is to blend the different aspects of your life together, not try to balance one against the other. It's up to you to figure out the needs and requirements of your home life and your work life and make them complement each other. This will create a fluid synergy among the various aspects of your life, rather than having them operate in opposition to one another. It will make you a congruent person, with your mind, body and soul all in sync.

---

[1] Morris R. Shechtman, *Working Without a Net: How to Survive and Thrive in Today's High-Risk Business World*, Simon & Schuster Inc., New York, 1994, pp. 18, 27, 75 and 152.

The Genius of the AND

A *scarcity mentality* tells us that we have only 24 hours in a day, and therefore we need to devote so many hours to this and so many hours to that, and that because we're doing one thing, we can't do another. An *abundance mentality* allows us to multitask. There are times — for example, after the kids are asleep — when you can get back on your computer and do the things you left at the office. It is, as Collins and Porras say in *Built to Last*, the genius of the AND, not the tyranny of the OR.[2] Maintain a positive mental attitude that you can accomplish many things by blending them together. And remember, they don't erect monuments to pessimists.

My hero in this regard is Ed Deutschlander, an executive vice president at North Star. How he accomplishes everything he does constantly amazes me. He has never missed any of his son's wrestling or karate matches or football games or any of his daughter's soccer matches, and they're both great athletes. Yet he does everything GAMA asks him to do as a member of the Executive Committee and everything North Star needs him to do. And he's a wonderful family man. He gets it all done because he believes in "the genius of the AND." Ed quotes Kemmons Wilson, the founder of Holiday Inn, who said he only works half days, with the only question being whether he works the first 12 hours or the last.[3]

Ed has a positive mental attitude that says, "I can blend all these things together and figure out how to do all of them." He's not trying to balance things against one another; he's trying to integrate them into a total Ed that gets everything done. Because he doesn't try to balance the various components of his life, they're never "out of balance." His many responsibilities do not take away from one another or oppose one another in a balancing act; they enhance and propel each other, drawing energy and momentum from one another. Admittedly, Ed is a special guy, but this mindset can be

---
[2]Jim C. Collins and Jerry I. Porras, *Built to Last: Successful Habits of Visionary Companies*, HarperCollins Publishers Inc., New York, 1997, pp. 43–45.
[3]Alan R. Zimmerman, *Pivot: How One Simple Turn in Attitude Can Lead to Success*, Peak Performance Publishers, Austin, Texas, 2006, p. 142.

contagious. Ed's success with such a well-blended life makes him a role model to everyone who knows him.

The best-adjusted advisors I have coached are those who believe in this blended approach. They believe that they have enough time for all the components of their lives, so one aspect of life doesn't dominate.

Our most contented, successful advisors know that if something is not right in one key area of their life, it will affect every other area. They think, "I've got to work hard in terms of my home life to make sure I have a successful business, and vice versa." The corollary to this concept is that when they vacation, they vacation; and when they're at work, they're at work. In other words, they don't vacation at the office. Because they're not worried about balancing different aspects of their life, they can focus completely on the moment.

Don't Fight the Tape
There's an old saying in the brokerage business: "Don't fight the tape." If the ticker tape dropped 200 points today and is continuing to drop, and you say, "Now is the time to buy," you're fighting the tape. You need to understand the situation for what it is. If that purchase is part of a thoughtful buying strategy, that's one thing; but impulse buying because stocks appear to be on sale is quite different. Impulse actions often lead to disappointment and frustration.

We need to understand things as they are and not as we would like them to be. For example, if one of my personal relationships is strained, that "tape" is going down, and I'm going to take it to work with me. If I fight that and don't recognize and correct it, it will introduce negativity into other aspects of my life. The first thing I should do, rather than internalize it, is share it with other people who are going to be affected by it. If I keep it to myself, that internalization will cause stress. The Italians have a proverb: "The Pope and the pauper know more than the Pope." If other people know what's going on in your life, they can offer resources, ideas and support that you may not have on your own at that moment.

On the other hand, if my work life is going well, the "tape" is going up, and the positive energy from that success will cast a positive light onto other aspects of my life.

Jim Benson, while moderating a Joint Executives Committee meeting of the major field organizations in our industry a few years ago, used the metaphor of "moving with the buffalo." Jim effectively made the case that, as industry leaders, we need to understand the changing environment and embrace it. He explained that the Native Americans who relied on the buffalo for food, clothing and shelter followed certain nomadic patterns because of the wisdom they had gleaned over centuries of moving with the buffalo. If you move too fast, you starve or freeze to death. If you move too slowly, the same fate awaits you. You must move with the buffalo to survive and thrive.

When Someone Is Struggling

If someone is dealing with a very serious issue, it's probably keeping him awake at night. This one aspect of his life is affecting all the other aspects. Sometimes he wakes up in the middle of the night thinking about it; sometimes it's the first thing on his mind when he wakes up in the morning; and sometimes he can't get to sleep at night because it's the last thing he's thinking about. We all struggle with difficult issues from time to time. Those times aren't fun.

Our responsibility as servant leaders is to recognize when someone is struggling — fighting the tape — and help him. My approach is to ask that person if he has a few minutes to spend with me, and I invite him into my office. Then I begin the conversation by asking a few open-ended questions.

During this process, I never mention production but instead ask questions such as these: "How are things going with you? What are the issues that are keeping you up at night? What would you change if you could?" The person may begin by talking about work, but he usually gets to any personal issues in short order.

When this happens, the person knows that I'm inquiring not because of his production but because I truly care about him as a human being, and this awareness allows, even compels, him to open up. That's what people who are dealing with problems are looking for — the chance to open up and get feedback, advice, wisdom and ideas. They're looking to express how they're feeling, and they're looking for someone who has been there before to listen. They're searching. That's why they're hurting, and that's why their production may be down and their relationships may be suffering. That downward spiral must be interrupted.

The best way to teach concepts like this is by example. Values are caught, not taught, and every member of our leadership team walks that talk. The next time that person is struggling, he will be more inclined to come to one of us directly because we've broken down some barriers and shown that we are genuinely concerned.

> *When personal and professional lives are integrated, values are more easily clarified.*
>
> Morrie Shechtman

You Take the Helm

- **Coach a Blended Approach** — Help your advisors lead fuller, less stressful lives by coaching them to *blend* the various aspects of their lives — home, work, health, spirituality, community involvement — instead of trying to *balance* them against each other.

- **Be Realistic** — A person's personal life will affect his or her professional life, and vice versa.

- **Address Stressors Openly; Don't Internalize Them** — Coach your advisors that the blended approach to life and work requires that they share bad news with other people who are going to be affected by it. This helps them build relationships and expands their support system. The truth does set us free.

- **Help Those Who Are Struggling** — If you see that someone is having a difficult time, speak to that person privately and ask open-ended questions. Worry, like rocking in a chair, gives our advisors something to do but gets them nowhere. Eliminate Excedrin® headaches by asking open-ended questions in closed-door meetings.

- **Don't Fight the Tape; Instead, Move with the Buffalo** — Understand your constantly changing environment and embrace it.

Chapter 13

Goals Change Behavior

IN 1979, RESEARCHERS asked the graduates of the MBA program at Harvard University if they had set clear, written goals for their future and made plans to accomplish them. Analysis of the graduates' responses revealed that 84 percent of them had no specific goals at all, aside from getting out of school and enjoying the summer; 13 percent had goals, but not in writing; and only 3 percent had written goals and plans.

Ten years later, the researchers interviewed the same graduates again and discovered that the 13 percent who had goals that were not in writing were earning, on average, twice as much as the 84 percent who had no goals at all. Further, they found that the 3 percent of graduates who had clear, written goals when they left Harvard were earning, on average, 10 times as much as the other 97 percent of graduates. The only difference between the groups was the clarity of the goals they had for themselves when they graduated.[1]

---
[1] Mark McCormack, *What They Don't Teach You at Harvard Business School*, cited in Brian Tracy, *Goals! How to Get Everything You Want—Faster than You Ever Thought Possible*, 2003, Berrett-Koehler Publishers, Inc., San Francisco, p. 12.

Effective goal setting can change people's behavior drastically.

One of my favorite stories about the impact that setting goals can have on a person's behavior comes from a classic audio presentation that I heard in 1963 by Dr. Bob Richards, the "pole-vaulting preacher." He was called that because he won an Olympic gold medal in pole vaulting and later became a Church of the Brethren minister. In his presentation, "The Higher Goals of Life," Dr. Richards described in detail the power of goals in both sports and life. He said, "If you want to accomplish in sport or any realm of life, you've got to set a goal — a high one. You've got to keep your eye on that goal, and you've got to follow through with all you've got." He closed his presentation with the following story.

Columbia University was playing another Ivy League team for the football championship. Four days before the championship game, Columbia's coach, Lou Little, picked up a telegram at the athletic department for a young man who had tried but couldn't quite make the team for four straight years. The telegram reported that this young man's only living relative had died. So the coach delivered the telegram to that young man. The kid looked at Lou Little and said, "Coach, I'll be back for Saturday's game."

On the morning of the game, the kid came up to his coach and said, "I want you to put me in this game. I know I haven't made the first team yet, but let me in for this kickoff. I'll prove to you that I'm worthy of it." Little could see that the kid was emotionally distraught, and he made all kinds of excuses to avoid letting him play. Finally he thought, "Well, he can't do much harm on the kickoff. I'll put the boy in."

As the crowd roared on the kickoff, the boy tackled the opposing team's receiver on the seven-yard line. So Little left the kid in for the next play, and he made the next tackle, and the next. He made practically every tackle and was the reason why Columbia won the championship that day.

Afterwards, all the guys were pounding the kid on the back in congratulations. When they were all done, Lou Little went up to him and said, "Son, I don't understand it. Today you were an All-

American. I've never seen you play like this in four straight years. What happened?"

The boy looked up at his coach and said, "Well, Coach, you knew my Dad died, didn't you?"

He said, "Yes, I handed you the telegram."

The kid said, "You know he was blind, don't you, Coach?"

Little said, "Yeah, I saw you walking him around the campus many times."

The kid replied, "Coach, this was the first football game my dad ever saw me play."

It is obvious that this young man had a goal, and it changed his behavior drastically. No one knows whether that young man had committed his goal to writing, but we do know that he had a goal, that it was lofty and that it worked.

I first heard that tape when I was an advisor at Maury Stewart's agency. I took it to my wrestling coach at Temple University, John Rogers, who was also the line coach on our football team. John played the tape at halftime of our game with the U.S. Coast Guard Academy. John later told me that the team was so moved by the story that they literally took the locker-room door off its hinges the wrong way on their way out to the field to defeat the Academy. Touch another man's sensitivity and he is capable of anything.

Put Your Goals in Writing

As the Harvard study indicated, having goals can help you double your results, but writing those goals down can multiply your results tenfold.

Our experience has also shown that people who commit their goals and plans to writing and refer to them frequently are far more likely to achieve them than the people who don't write their goals down. We have found that those advisors and managers who work from well-thought-out business plans end up among the top 20 percent of productive units in any business model, producing 80 percent of the results. (This is another example of the 80–20 rule, which we discuss in Chapter 17.)

Committing to written goals is something I do in my personal life as well. In 2001, I had a new goal to bicycle 100 miles in a week, something I had never done on my mountain bike. As of Thursday night, I had logged 88 miles. The next morning, I had an 8 a.m. flight to Dallas for a meeting, to be followed on Saturday morning with another flight to Montreal for another meeting. So I planned to rise at 3 a.m. on Friday and bike the 12 miles I needed to make my 100-mile goal before I left for the airport, knowing that Friday would be my last chance in the week to hit the goal.

Committing to this written goal motivated me to get up at 3 a.m. as planned. I came up out of the underground garage in the dead of night with no lights on my bike to a heavy thunderstorm and torrential rain. I biked for the next hour in the dark and in the rain. If I had not had a written goal that I had committed to, that simply would not have happened.

At North Star, we take it even one step further by encouraging people to put their goals in the public domain. Goals that are kept secret are devoid of accountability. We know that achieving a goal elicits in us the same "high" that winning a contest does. If no one knows that we are competing, then there can be no high-fives when we win.

This phenomenon of putting our goals into the public view and out of our own private domain drastically improves the probability that they will be achieved. Athletes perform better on game day than they do in the wrestling room or on the practice field. World records occur in competition and rarely in practice. The stage makes the difference.

Goals enable you to accomplish things that you otherwise might consider unattainable. Convince your advisors, especially the new ones, of that maxim, and you'll improve your retention rate and their performance.

Set Big, Hairy, Audacious Goals

I first learned about the term "BHAG" — big, hairy, audacious goals — in *Built to Last*. In that book, authors Collins and Porras define a

BHAG as a commitment to challenging, audacious and often risky goals and projects toward which a visionary company channels its efforts. They go on to explain that having BHAGs is one specific method of stimulating the progress that distinguished the visionary companies from the comparison companies.[2]

Coca-Cola was one of the visionary companies that Collins and Porras studied. After assuming his role as chairman of the board and CEO of Coca-Cola on March 1, 1981, Roberto Goizueta publicized his carefully crafted "Strategy for the 1980s."[3] One of the things he preached to worldwide audiences of Coca-Cola employees was that the human body requires 64 ounces of liquid every day. "Our beverages currently account for not even two of those ounces," he lamented. "Go get the other 62!"[4]

During the 1980s, Coca-Cola's stock appreciated more than 735 percent, creating some $30 billion in additional stockholder wealth and more than doubling the performance of the S&P 500 index. The company sold more than 45 percent of all of the world's carbonated soft drinks, more than double Pepsi's record.[5]

That's a perfect example of a BHAG made public. Writing down his call to action and publicizing it energized and defined the goal. If Goizueta had kept that goal to himself, Coca-Cola no doubt would have been in the "comparison" group of companies.

In 1990, I set the BHAG for North Star to be the largest independent financial-planning organization in the world, as measured by GAMA International. At that time, I don't think we were even in the top 50. In 2005, North Star was ranked number two overall and first among independent firms.

---

[2]Jim Collins and Jerry I. Porras, *Built to Last: Successful Habits of Visionary Companies,* 1994 and 1997, HarperCollins Publishers Inc.: New York, p. 89.
[3]Mark Pendergrast, *For God, Country, and Coca-Cola: The Definitive History of the Great American Soft Drink and the Company that Makes It,* 2000, Basic Books: New York, p. 336.
[4]Pendergrast, p. 410.
[5]Pendergrast, p. 388.

Goals as Life-Sustaining Focal Points

Not only can BHAGs help us achieve outstanding success; they also can help us survive life-threatening trauma. My dear friend John Michael McGrath has more character than any other person I've ever met, and he has accomplished amazing goals despite a haunting six-year ordeal in a Vietnamese POW camp that could easily have ended his life.

I met Mike McGrath on a wrestling mat in Philadelphia at Temple University when we were both sophomores. Mike wrestled for the U.S. Naval Academy, and his coach was a guy named Ray Schwartz. My coach at Temple University was John Rogers.

The biggest goal of my lifetime was to attend the U.S. Naval Academy in Annapolis. I had dreamed about this goal since I was five years old. Schwartz had recruited me to the Naval Academy. In fact, my high school wrestling coach, John Maitland, was convinced that the reason I did not win the state wrestling championship in Pennsylvania was because I was taking the entrance exam to get into Annapolis. I had taken and passed the physical exam already, and I had already secured the required principalship from a Congressman to attend the U.S. Naval Academy. I failed the exam by three points. So not only did I forfeit a probable state championship in Pennsylvania, but I didn't get into Annapolis, either. That was in 1958. What a bummer, I thought.

If I had taken that exam in 1957 or in 1959, I would have passed with flying colors with the score I got in 1958. But in 1957, Russia launched the Sputnik. The U.S. Naval Academy, an engineering school, panicked in light of that competition from Russia. So they decided to raise the entrance-exam requirement by 50 points.

In 1959, the Naval Academy lowered the entrance score by 50 points, back to what it had been in 1957, but my fate had been sealed by that time.

When we found out that I did not get into Annapolis, Coach Schwartz wanted to send me to Columbian Preparatory School in Washington, D.C., and then have me attend the Naval Academy after one year there, but I did not want to lose the year. So I put my name back out there, and soon other schools found out that I was available. All of a sudden, I had many scholarship offers, and I accepted the one from Temple. As with so many things in life, we have to play the cards we're dealt.

Schwartz brought his team up to Philadelphia to wrestle Temple. Navy beat us 26–3. I got Temple the 3 points by beating Mike McGrath 5–4 on riding time — it was 4–4 at the end of regulation. I had controlled him more than a minute longer than he had controlled me, so I got a point and bested him. But Mike almost broke my neck, and he put an early end to my sophomore year. That match with Mike left me with a slipped disc, a torn trapezius and complications from those injuries. I spent the next eight weeks in a neck brace not knowing whether Mike had ended just my season or my entire wrestling career.

The next year, Temple went down to the U.S. Naval Academy to wrestle in Halsey Hall. I was slated to meet Mike McGrath again in the 147-pound weight division.

That day, the proverbial weenie bird made an appearance. That's the bird that flies in ever-decreasing concentric circles until it flies up its own behind, and that's what our two coaches did that fateful day.

Coach Schwartz did not want Mike McGrath to ever wrestle me again because he thought I could beat him again. My coach, Rogers, didn't want me to wrestle Mike again. He thought I had been lucky to beat him in riding time the previous year and didn't want me to lose and run the risk of sustaining more injuries in a new match with him.

So both coaches tried to outsmart the other. Schwartz had McGrath slim down to 137 pounds from 147, which was the fighting weight we had both previously been at, so that he and I would be in different categories. But my coach did the same thing! He sent me down to 137 because he didn't want me to meet McGrath at 147. There we both were, at 137 pounds.

When you weigh in for a wrestling match, you wait for your school, weight and name to be called, at which time you remove your robe and step onto the scale, stark naked, since every gram of weight matters. The referee then presides over the weigh-in.

The home team has to field its candidate first. So the referee called out, "One-thirty-seven. U.S. Naval Academy. Michael McGrath." My coach turned white when he heard Mike's name called in the 137-pound group. He realized that he had outsmarted himself. I could see the blood drain from his face as this realization hit him.

Then they called the guest team: "Temple University. One-thirty-seven. Phil Richards." Schwartz turned white. These two guys were beside themselves. They had both come up with the same strategy, and it didn't work because they both did it. If only one had done it, it would have marked a genius.

So I stepped onto the scale, and instead of weighing 137, I missed weight by two and a quarter pounds. I was over, at 139.25 pounds. Technically, that meant that Mike McGrath won by forfeit, which is the same as a "pin" in wrestling parlance, and the U.S. Naval Academy would have started the match with a five-point lead.

But the story didn't end there. Mike McGrath came up to me and said, "We have five hours before the match. The Navy has just come up with some new fiberglass uniforms that don't breathe. We can roll around in the wrestling room until you lose the two and a quarter pounds. And then we can go through with the match."

Instead of walking away with his win, Mike wanted to go through with the match and take a chance on losing. He gave the automatic win away. He wanted to beat me because he was a competitor and a true champion. He was also willing to use up his precious energy sparring with me for the principle of the thing.

That was the most character-laden act I have ever seen in the athletic world. Mike is a true warrior.

Since then, many people have said to me, "Phil, you would have done the same thing." But I am here to tell you that I would not have. I'm not being humble; I'm being truthful. I would not have done that. And I don't know too many people who would have done that. It was an amazing act by a very special person.

So Mike and I wrestled around in the 120-degree wrestling room for several hours, and I miraculously made the weight. It was another tough match. I beat Mike 4–2, and Navy beat Temple 23–6. In that match, Mike broke my sternum, but of course I didn't let him know about it. My competitive nature prevented me from admitting that, in fact, he had really won that day. That injury, like the one a year earlier, ended my season. The scoreboard displayed a different winner from the real one. Mike again went on to successfully compete in the post-season tournaments, no doubt wondering where I was.

I could never get that amazing thing that Mike did out of my mind. Sometime later, I wrote him a letter to tell him how I felt about his act and what a real star he was. He wrote me a letter back. We corresponded a couple more times. Then all of a sudden, he did not respond anymore, and my letter came back.

I later found out that Mike graduated from the Naval Academy in 1962 and completed his obligatory five years of service. When he finished the Naval Academy, he had applied to the U.S. Marine Corps so that he could become a pilot assigned to an aircraft carrier. He was accepted, flew for the next few years and then resigned his Navy commission at the end of the five-year period.

Mike's lifelong dream had been to become a professional airline pilot, not to graduate from the U.S. Naval Academy, as I had wanted to do.

In 1967, Mike applied to United Airlines to become a pilot and fulfill his lifelong goal. He passed their physical exam and some additional tests. He was about ready to go in for his final interview when President Lyndon Johnson issued an involuntary recall of military troops who had resigned their commissions, reactivating their military service status.

Mike McGrath was one of those people. He was immediately reactivated into the Navy, was put on an aircraft carrier to Vietnam and couldn't communicate with anybody.

On his 179th mission over North Vietnam, Mike was shot down. He recalled that his parachute opened only a few feet above the treetops. During those few seconds in the chute, he vowed that someday he would return to his country and his family. He was injured in that landing. Soon he was captured by the North Vietnamese, who injured him further by stepping on his arm and breaking it during interrogation and denying him medical treatment.

Mike's goal sustained him through six years of brutal captivity. His character, honor and determination to survive helped him endure unthinkable atrocities.

Mike was in the same prison camp as John McCain, the Republican Senator from Arizona. Mike chronicled his years in captivity in a book that he wrote and illustrated, *Prisoner of War — Six Years in Hanoi*.

Mike is a wonderful artist. During his time as a POW, he made amazing charcoal drawings of the torture that he and his comrades endured on toilet tissue using cigarette ashes and tiny sticks.

The way that I reconnected with Mike is quite a coincidence. One of my partners in a sailboat in San Diego, George Leonard, also graduated from the U.S. Naval Academy in 1962. He did not personally know John Michael McGrath, even though they had been in the same class, but he said, "I can find him for you." And he did.

Mike and I renewed our relationship, and then for years, we had a number of conversations on the phone but never got together in person until 1998, when Minnesota Mutual had its meeting for managing partners in Colorado Springs, where Mike lives. He brought his wife, Marlene, to dinner. I was with Terry Sullivan, who was the senior vice president of Minnesota Mutual, and Dick Lee, who was a first vice president for Minnesota Mutual. Dick had also graduated in 1962 from the U.S. Naval Academy and flew missions over North Vietnam, but he had never met Mike.

That night at dinner, I confessed to Mike that he had broken my sternum 40 years earlier during our final wrestling match at the U.S. Naval Academy and that he had ended the previous season for me as well with another injury that required a neck brace for eight weeks. The confession that pride had prevented me from making for all those years finally came out. I brought myself around to admitting the irony that here was a contestant who thought he had lost but had really won, and another contestant who thought he had won but had really lost. Twice!

Also that night, I introduced Mike McGrath and Dick Lee to one another. In a conversation that should be included in Ripley's "Believe It or Not," Mike and Dick determined that they indeed had been flying missions over Vietnam for six months on the same aircraft carrier but had never met.

Throughout his ordeal, Mike had never forgotten his dream. After he was freed from captivity and came back home, he wrote a letter to United Airlines and said, "I'm ready to come in for my final interview."

They wrote him back and said, "We have no record of you. Can you clear this up?"

He sent them his applicant number.

They called him and said, "We haven't used that number in decades. What's this all about?"

Mike explained what happened, and United Airlines hired him as a commercial pilot at age 52, making him the oldest person they had ever appointed as a pilot. Good things do indeed happen to good people.

Goals change behavior, and they give people a reason to keep forging ahead, even through dire circumstances. In the end, character wins.

Incidentally, Mike is the only veteran who was ever asked to stay on for a second term as president of the NAM-POWS, a national organization that is composed of all 660 Vietnam-era POWs who got out alive from Laos, Cambodia, China, and South and North Vietnam.

When Our Goals Are Thwarted

We don't always accomplish our goals, regardless of how determined we are. I'm not sure that I have fully gotten over, to this very day, the fact that I failed to achieve my boyhood dream of going to Annapolis.

But having my life take a different direction has resulted in other, more meaningful, benefits and blessings. I probably would not have met and married my wonderful wife, Sue, if I had gone to Annapolis. My children wouldn't be. And I almost certainly wouldn't be in the life insurance business that has rewarded me so richly in too many ways to count.

But losing does hurt. And we are hardwired to avoid pain whenever possible. So we must do whatever we are capable of doing to avoid losing but, at the same time, accept the final outcome and realize that in the end, we may, in fact, have fared better than we otherwise might have had we accomplished the goal that we originally set out to achieve.

Dr. Bob Richards said that we can have victory in defeat. Life is full of frustrating times when we give all we've got and still don't make our goal. He said, "In the striving, in the development of a will that can run down that deep, a man is learning a great lesson about life, that somehow there can be more victory in a striving like that than there is in victory itself." And he gave a personal example. He said that he fell two and a half inches short of his goal to pole-vault 15 feet, 8.5 inches. But having that goal had a tremendous impact on his life, gave every chin-up and every moment of weight lifting true meaning and led to his ultimate success as an Olympic gold medalist.

Whatever our outcome as field leaders, we can make the most of our situation by committing to lifelong learning, servant leadership, hard work, smart work, empowering others and leveraging ourselves through them, sharing best practices through study groups and the LAMP experience and living with like-minded people.

And we can coach and lead our advisors to set their sights high and to help them make the most of their circumstances, even if they do not accomplish a specific goal. As a wise person once observed, we cannot control the direction of the wind, but we can adjust our sails.

Life is not a silent auction but rather a stage on which our dreams with deadlines, our goals, give us a sense of pride when we accomplish them or another mountain to climb when we fail to accomplish them. Failures are not those individuals who lose but those who stop trying. Successful individuals are not those who win but those who are on a journey of successive achievements as a result of refusing to quit.

> *Man is a goal-seeking animal. His life only has meaning if he is reaching out and striving for his goals.*
> ARISTOTLE

You Take the Helm

- **Define Your Goals** — Increase your chances of reaching your goals by defining them and writing them down.

- **Put Your Goals in the Public Domain** — When others know what you are striving for, they can support your efforts and celebrate your successes.

- **Accept Outcomes** — Realize that every locked door opens other opportunities. If you do not accomplish a goal, make the most of your circumstances, and recognize the alternative benefits that you have acquired along your new path. Teach your advisors to do the same.

- **Nurture Your Relationships** — With all your might, hang onto those relationships with people you want to emulate. You will become more like them with each passing day.

Chapter 14

Habits

All You Need Is 30 Days and a Commitment

AS A WRESTLER, I learned a lot about forming habits. I was an "unconscious competent" in that respect, because I didn't realize just how much I knew.

In wrestling, I quickly learned that certain things must be done every day. Push-ups, chin-ups, long runs, drills and stair climbing had to be offered up seven days a week. I knew these were habits I had to get into if I wanted my team to win. Being strong and determined is no competitive advantage when everyone else is strong and determined. You need a competitive advantage.

So even before coming into this great business, I knew that habits are like ruts in a muddy road. But I also realized early on that ruts can be either good or bad. If you're in a bad habit, you're confronted with the necessity of breaking it. Smoking, swearing — whatever the bad habit is — you've got to break out of that rut and, as you know from driving on rutted roads, that's easier said than done.

When I was first hired into Maury Stewart's organization, he introduced me to a concept made famous by Earl Nightingale, who was for decades one of the country's foremost personal development gurus. In 1959, Nightingale produced an unbelievably successful audio recording titled "The Strangest Secret for Being Successful in the World Today." In it, he talked about forming habits. He said that if you do something every day for 30 days, it will own you, you will own it and it will be very comfortable for you from that point on. But you've got to do it 30 days in a row. That's the tough part. After 30 days, it's second nature.

Helping New Advisors Develop Good Habits
We've expanded Nightingale's 30-day model. We want our new advisors to develop good habits. New advisors need and deserve a lot of attention, and we must inculcate the proper habits into them at the outset. Remember, during the first 90 days, they'll do anything you tell them to do but very little of what you tell them to do thereafter.

I recently addressed a group of new advisors and used a Picasso lithograph as a prop. (Collecting lithographs is one of my hobbies.) This lithograph, from Picasso's later works, looks like something a kindergartener drew. There are people with eyes coming out of the sides of their heads, people with their legs twisted and on backwards and other very strange depictions. People look at something like this and ask, "How could that be a $100,000 piece of art?" What many people don't know about Picasso is that he could duplicate a Rembrandt painting freehand so well that only an expert could tell the difference between the original and Picasso's copy.

Picasso's art underwent many transformations over his lifetime. He could paint anything he wanted. Later in his career, he selected a more daring, less colorful and more expressive style.

My message to the new advisors is that before Picasso painted this seemingly whimsical piece, he first got to the place where he could paint anything. It was because of all his accumulated wisdom, experience and talent that he felt free to use such a unique style.

Dali, Chagall and Miro made the same kind of transformation in their careers. Miro was reported to have said, "I spent my whole life learning to paint like a child."

So I explain to our new advisors that we're going to force them to do things our way in the beginning. Someday they'll be able to add their own creativity and talent to financial planning. But they have to know how to paint a Rembrandt first; they have to know the right way to do things. They have to be professionals first. Our clients deserve no less.

In their first 90 days at North Star, we ask new advisors to be smart enough to trust us. We ask for faith. We want them to do things because we tell them to, because we know how to bring them from where they are now — which is apprehensive — to being successful financial advisors. That's what we're good at. That's what we do. The shoemaker makes good shoes because that's the only thing he makes.

Like the Marine Corps does in officer training camp, we require our new advisors to do things our way; once they're successful, they can do things their way. What we're really expecting them to do is to buy into the concepts that will ensure their success. As Al Granum, one of my fellow Management Hall of Famers, says, "If you're going to fail around here, you're going to fail my way." In Chapter 8, we talked about those concepts and said that the critical number for a new advisor is a minimum of 30 appointments on the books at all times. That's our way. After advisors qualify for MDRT, they can do it their way.

You can't control results, but you can control activity. Al Granum's One Card System continues to prove that after 40 years. As Maury Stewart repeated frequently, "Neither the system nor the life insurance business is on trial; you are."

In addition to having at least 30 appointments on the books, we want to create habits in our advisors for participating in telephone drills and always — not sometimes, not when they feel like it, but always — being on the lookout for centers of influence and referred leads. We know they are capable of doing these things because that's what we tested and interviewed for and that's what they said they could do and what they committed to do when we hired them.

We teach them the systems to succeed, and the key to their success is in the execution. It isn't about them; it's about the execution of systems that work. Those systems will set them free and give them time to do the things they enjoy doing.

In the first 90 days, we want our new advisors to develop the right habits because we know that after 90 days, they're going to do very little of what we ask them to do. If they develop the right habits during the first 90 days, we know they'll continue to do those things over the long term. They're in a rut, but it's a good rut. That's why developing good habits is so critical during those first 90 days.

Our new advisors must commit to the standards that have been designed for them. They're told that they must *commit* to doing the things we require them to do in their first 90 days. It's not enough for them just to be *involved* — they must be committed.

When discussing commitment, I remind advisors of the World War II kamikaze pilot who flew 99 missions. That pilot was involved, but he certainly wasn't committed. If he had been committed, he would have met his maker on his first mission. To fly 99 missions without effect is involvement. Our business is too challenging to succeed in by merely being involved.

The people who will succeed and rise to the top will make that commitment: "I'll do what I need to do to be successful in this business." In the beginning, they don't know what needs to be done. We do know. We've done it. This is not guesswork for us. We specialize in bringing people from feelings of apprehension to a predictable path to success.

Into Good Ruts, Out of Bad Ruts

It is a blessing to be in a good habit, or rut. The following two personal stories will help make my point.

In 1995, I decided to read the Bible cover to cover, both the Old and New Testaments. Having been brought up memorizing the Baltimore Catechism, this would be a first for me. It took a year. I read one chapter each day. That was the deal — to do it every morning. I realized that it would be easy to maintain the habit once I got in the rut, and I've now been in that rut for more than a decade. Each day, I read one chapter in the Bible. Friends say, "Boy, that's really amazing." It's not amazing at all. If you're in a rut, you do it automatically. You don't even think about it. You're on cruise control.

The second rut I'm in is completing seven hours a week of exercise, whether it's biking, riding a stationary bike, using an elliptical machine or taking a power walk with my wife, Sue. I add it up using a runner's watch — 28 15-minute segments each and every week. I've been doing this for 15 years. I keep a cumulative year-to-date tally of my total exercise time and log my results every Saturday morning in an appointment book.

Goals must be written down, measured and managed. Goals that we commit to writing are powerful motivators. As I said in Chapter 13, goals change behavior, and when you change your behavior, it's very easy to develop good habits.

Just as the key to developing a good habit is to do it for 30 days in a row, the key to breaking a bad habit is to refrain from doing it for 30 days in a row.

As everyone knows, one of the worst ruts a person can be in is smoking. Physicians tell us that smoking is more than just a psychological habit; it's a physiological addiction as well. For that reason, it's more difficult to quit smoking for 30 consecutive days than it is to kick other habits. But the commitment aspect is still applicable.

Many people die of lung cancer after spending most of their lives trying to break the smoking habit. My heart goes out to them because stopping smoking was the single toughest thing I've had to do in my lifetime. I tried and failed more than a hundred times. Throughout my many failures, I always consoled myself by saying, "I only have to win once. If I have one win and 130 losses, I win." As with most efforts in life, we don't always win, but we have unlimited opportunities to try. Losers quit, but winners never stop trying.

Smoking a couple of packs of cigarettes a day was my addiction. I was unable to quit even after participating in a five-day hospital program. But my failure did not prevent me from continuing to try. The critical tipping point occurred when I was 37 years old, with the birth of my daughter, Christina. The baby provided me with the extra motivation I needed — having secondary smoke around her was unacceptable. It was not about me; it was about understanding the rules of engagement that apply to us all.

Is there anything scientific or magical about the 30-day time frame for beginning or ending a habit? I don't know. I just know that Earl Nightingale said it, and I believe it. I did what we're asking our new advisors to do — and that is to be smart enough to just listen and try it. Faith works.

> *Habit is either the best of servants or the worst of masters.*
> NATHANIEL EMMONS

You Take the Helm

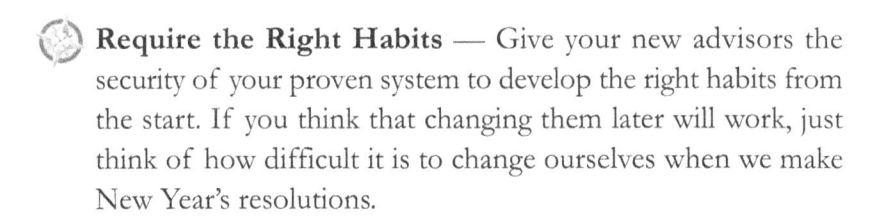

- **Require the Right Habits** — Give your new advisors the security of your proven system to develop the right habits from the start. If you think that changing them later will work, just think of how difficult it is to change ourselves when we make New Year's resolutions.

- **Give It 30 Days** — Develop a new habit by doing it for 30 days in a row, and break a bad habit by not doing it for 30 days in a row. Understand that the pain of discipline is less than the pain of regret.

- **Have Faith** — Faith may not cure cancer, but it does rank up there with food and oxygen.

- **Encourage Faith** — Require your advisors to put their faith in you for 90 days. By then, they probably will have developed the habits they need to succeed.

- **Create a Cruise-Control Practice** — Coach your advisors to develop the habits and systems that can put their practices on cruise control. That will free their time to do the things they enjoy doing.

- **Be Fully Committed** — Commit to doing the right thing. It's not enough just to be involved. Remember, winners don't always win, but unlike losers, they never stop trying.

Chapter 15

20,000 Rejections

HAVING RETURNED recently from a visit to China and Thailand, I can still almost feel the constant pummeling at the bazaars and markets. If you have experienced it, you know what it's like to meander down the aisles filled with zealous young vendors who are selling everything from knock-off Gucci bags and Swiss watches to DVDs and polo shirts.

With my runner's watch, I timed the assaults at 51 in a single minute. If you do the math, that means that I might have fended off as many as 7,000 solicitations in my two-and-a-half-hour shopping journey.

This experience made me think about our advisors and the thousands of rejections that each of them endures over the course of their first few years in the business. This rejection challenge clearly contributes heavily to the 87 percent failure rate in our industry and 36 percent four-year retention rate at our firm.

To succeed in this business, an advisor needs 300 clients. Using Al Granum's 10:3:1 model, an advisor needs 10 suspects to get three prospects to get one client. So an advisor will have to make presentations to 3,000 suspects; 900 of them will become prospects; and, finally, 300 of those — only 1.5 percent of the total number of people the advisor originally spoke with — will become clients.

I've calculated that during the process of obtaining 300 clients, an advisor will get approximately 20,000 rejections, either on the phone or in person. The best salesperson in the world may be able to obtain 300 clients after only 15,000 rejections. And the worst salesperson might get to that goal with 25,000 rejections. But give or take 5,000 rejections, it will take 20,000 rejections for advisors to obtain the 300 clients that they will serve in this business.

Controlling the Duration of the Pain

Advisors have no control over the number of rejections. We don't make the rules of life, but we are responsible for knowing what they are. There is, however, one thing that is totally within their control: the duration of the pain. Stated differently, advisors can decide to get through all of the pain associated with those 20,000 rejections in the first three years of their career, then get a life and really begin to enjoy this business. Or they can stretch the pain out over 10 or 20 years. The unfortunate fact is that I've seen people who spend their entire career — 40 years — in pain because they still haven't been rejected 20,000 times.

So the one thing that advisors can control is how long they choose to suffer. That motivates many of our young advisors because they *get* it. They say, "Why would I want to stretch it out? I'm going to get all of this pain out of the way in a hurry." The more times we repeat this to our newer advisors, the more of them will throw themselves into the fray. It's fun to watch the lights go on, one at a time.

Videotape Everything

As managers, it's our job to help advisors endure those rejections and develop their sales skills, professionalism and confidence. One tactic we use at North Star is to videotape them.

We videotape their telephone approach, their referred-lead approach, their elevator talk (that 20- to 60-second speech they give when someone asks what they do) and their memorized presentations.

Helping advisors polish their presentations gives them the confidence they need to endure the rejections they will get in the early part of their career so that they won't become discouraged and leave without giving themselves a fair chance.

Here is an example of an effective elevator talk. In our business, working primarily with physicians, an advisor may meet a physician on an elevator. The physician might say, "What do you do?" The advisor will reply this way: "You know, physicians spend many years in school and training and then have limited time in which they can maximize their earnings. They generally don't start making money until they're in their mid-thirties, and they're usually very much in debt. What I do is help physicians reach their financial and retirement dreams in spite of their limited number of working years."

While that may seem long, if you time it you'll see that it takes less than 20 seconds to state. We have new advisors memorize that brief speech or one like it, and then we videotape them delivering it. We do this so that when the opportunity arises they're not focusing on what they're about to say. They're focusing on the reaction of the person they're saying it to.

Videotaping is a training strategy that gets people to see themselves and how they're coming across. Is their inflection right? Is their body language right? Are they communicating properly? Are their facial expressions reassuring? Are they stumbling over their words? How are they being perceived by someone else? It also gives the trainer an opportunity to look for improvement the second and third time the advisor is videotaped. We videotape them until they get it right. It's an exercise very much like drills performed on athletic practice fields when not in real competition.

Usually the videotaping takes place with just the trainer and the advisor isolated in a room. But we've also incorporated this experience into our peer-accountability meetings so that individuals take their turn delivering the talk in front of everyone. We purposely make the situation stressful because when they deliver this speech to a real suspect (perhaps on the elevator), it will be a stressful situation. If we have them practice "under glass," where there's no intimidation, then they will have a less effective presentation in front of an actual suspect.

Life After the 20,000 Rejections

Our objective for new advisors is for them to have those 300 clients in no more than five years. But attaining 300 clients doesn't mean that they can quit prospecting. At that point, they will continually upgrade the quality of their clientele.

A good rule of thumb is that the advisor's income will be the median income of all of his or her clients: if an advisor has 300 clients whose median income is $150,000, that advisor should expect to be very close to that income level. (We use the median instead of the average because a few clients at high income levels might skew the resulting number.) In the above example, the advisor should be trying to mentor a more junior advisor to start working with those clients who are below an income of $150,000. These clients would then move to that advisor's list of lower-tier clients (A or AA clients, as we discuss in Chapter 17), and he would mentor the junior advisor to take them over or work on the accounts on a split basis.

That will free up enough of the more experienced advisor's time to get more clients whose income is above $150,000. The way advisors obtain additional top-tier (AAA) clients is by asking for quality referrals from their existing clients. We address this next step of their career in our quarterly reviews with advisors. Here's an example of how that conversation might go.

I will say to the advisor, "Let me ask you this. Is there a common denominator among your 20 best clients?"

He might say, "Well, yes, they're all small-business owners."

"Great. OK. That means that you probably enjoy doing business with and being around small-business people. Is that right?"

"Right."

Then I tell the advisor that I want him to have 20 lunches over the next month, I want him to call up each of those 20 people and invite them to lunch. And here is what the advisor should tell each client: "This is not going to be a business luncheon, and it's not going to be a review of your portfolio. It is going to be a personal 'life note.' By a life note, I mean that I've really been thinking through my practice and where I want it to go. I did an analysis of my practice, and what I learned was that the people I really enjoy working with are also my best clients. The reason I called you for lunch is that you are one of those 20 people. The thing you have in common with the other 19 people is that you're a small-business owner. You're an entrepreneur. You work very hard and are very successful. You're serious about your future and about the continuation of your business if you were not here and the well-being of your family if you were gone. I've decided that I'm going to hand off those clients who do not meet that profile to other, newer people with less experience in our firm or to other advisors for whom these clients are a better fit. I'm going to focus on and specialize in people just like you. To do this, I'm going to need your help. I need you to identify and help me access people who are just like you — serious, successful, entrepreneurial business owners. Will you do that for me?"

Then the advisor should quit speaking and wait for a response.

Quality referrals are one of the substantial payoffs for having our advisors navigate their way through 20,000 rejections. Unlike the marketplace vendors, who will always be hawking their wares to the general public, our advisors are eventually rewarded with a loyal clientele that they can continually upgrade for the duration of their careers, thus increasing their enjoyment of work, standard of living and quality of life.

> *The secret of every man who has ever been successful lies in the fact that he formed a habit of doing the things failures don't like to do.*
>
> ALBERT GRAY

You Take the Helm

- **Help Advisors Navigate Inevitable Rejection** — Let your advisors know they must endure about 20,000 rejections in the process of obtaining 300 clients.

- **Teach the Relationship Between Income and Clientele** — A good rule of thumb is that a producer's income will be equal to the median income of his or her clients.

- **Help Advisors Prepare** — Great athletes are those who drill, drill, drill. Implement exercises that will help advisors polish their professional skills, such as videotaping their elevator talks. Bertrand R. Canfield said, "Successful salesmanship is 90 percent preparation and 10 percent presentation."

- **Coach Advisors to Upgrade Their Clientele** — Once advisors have attained 300 clients, coach them to upgrade their clientele. Have them identify the characteristic among their top 20 clients and then to ask them for referrals to other people who share that characteristic.

Chapter 16

Your Worst Deal Is Your Only Deal

A BUSINESS REFLECTS the values of its leader. If you are a servant leader, you will attract and retain a team of giving people in your organization. If money is your god, your business and your people will be greedy as well. Each business develops its individual culture either intentionally or as a result of those things it permits or prohibits. Once established, that culture will spit out those who demonstrate alien behavior.

Every organization is perfectly aligned to get the very results it gets. It's a logical argument — an organization's alignment produces its outcome, and that alignment begins with its leader.

If you want to change your organization, you must begin by looking at yourself, changing your habits, examining your values and then selecting a team of advisors who embrace or reflect those values.

We can improve ourselves by committing to lifelong learning and by maintaining high standards regarding whom we hire. That also means that we have to bite the bullet with C- and D-level players. We cannot keep underperformers simply because we have the space, reasoning that they're not doing any harm. They are doing harm. New hires will quickly learn the minimum acceptable level of performance in any organization and gravitate to that standard.

The way you handle compensation in your firm or agency is also a reflection of you as a leader. We set ourselves up for failure when we make special deals with certain advisors and say, "This is between you and me," expecting them to not share the information with others.

People Talk

Advisors have far more in common with one another than they have with you. So to assume that your special deal is not going to see the light of day is wishful thinking and a bad assumption. Your worst deal — a special deal you make with any one of your advisors — will become the only deal you have when other advisors hear about it. Of course, they will expect the same deal. And why shouldn't they?

For example, let's assume that we're paying 60 percent maximum commission to one of our advisors. Later that advisor says, "Unless you pay me 65 percent, I'm leaving," or "I am being offered 65 percent elsewhere, and I must think of my family first."

Our reaction might be, "OK, I'll pay you 65 percent, but this must stay between the two of us."

Now we have just made a special deal with that advisor, and it is the *worst* deal we have because our *best* deals are all 60 percent. The moment we pay — or say we're going to pay — one advisor 65 percent, that's going to become the only deal we've got because when other advisors find out about it, they're going to walk into our office and say, "I heard that you're paying him 65 percent. Unless you pay me the same thing you're paying him, I'm going to quit."

Those advisors will be mad at us because we treated them unfairly, and we will have lost their trust. They'll always wonder if they are being compensated fairly.

Everything is at stake when we make special deals — they compromise our personal integrity and the integrity of our processes, our model and ultimately our business results. While the above oversimplified example is about percentage payouts, the principle applies to both quantitative and qualitative rewards.

Cautioning managers about making special deals may seem unnecessary, but it isn't. I know many, many managers who have suffered because they did not follow this tenet. Compensation and rewards are very delicate subjects, and managers must be extremely careful how they communicate and apply them. This principle is no less true for team members or other office workers, though it is less pronounced because their results are generally less quantifiable in nature than the strict percentage amounts paid to advisors.

Fair, Not Equal

Fortunately, you don't have to treat people equally as long as you treat them fairly. You can design your compensation plan to reward those people who are creating your ability to increase that compensation, as long as you don't do it retroactively. Retroactive adjustments cause distrust in the integrity of your process and in your personal integrity.

In our case, we are barely making a profit on advisors at Million Dollar Round Table level. Advisors at MDRT level are at the bottom of our compensation grid. I would not say that is common. But the services in our firm are expensive — the fixed overhead in our firm in 2006 was $650,000 a month, not counting commissions. We have 23 salaried people on staff who are in management positions, and while they are very productive, they produce no business. We have in excess of 120,000 square feet of space throughout our system. We have an attorney and a CPA on staff who help our people do fee planning and tax returns. We have an in-house brokerage department, a policyholder service department, a marketing department, a compliance department, a four-person technical services department, a four-person employee benefits department, a securities assistance department and a training department. As one might imagine, a shop of this size has tremendous fixed expense loads.

In our firm, we encourage high performance because we know that we are going to get the results that we expect, and we compensate for them. So if advisors do twice MDRT level, which is approximately $150,000 of first-year commissions, they will receive a bonus on the second $75,000, meaning that they get a higher percentage on the second $75,000 than on the first $75,000. Now, if those advisors do Court of the Table, which is three times MDRT, they will receive an even greater percentage on the third $75,000.

Publish your compensation schedule, and be sure that everybody gets the same deal. Design your compensation plan on a level playing field with aggregated payouts based on a high-performance, no-excuse model. Design it so that you can explain it and demonstrate that everybody has exactly the same deal. In this way, you create not only an unassailable compensation grid, but also a transparent environment that creates trust in the system and the organization.

Then, when a producer says, "I'm getting 55 percent with my bonuses, but Joan is getting 65 percent. Why is she getting more?" you can truthfully answer, "Her compensation is exactly the same as yours, and she is getting 65 percent only on the amount above MDRT — the amount between $75,000 and $150,000. She's getting 55 percent on the amounts from zero to $75,000, just the same as you are. I am anxious to pay you the higher amounts just as soon as you perform at the higher level, which, as we have discussed often, you are more than capable of."

In this way, you mitigate the rumor mill and eliminate the potential for people to be legitimately disgruntled. In a model where you incrementally increase compensation, bonuses or expense allowances beyond a certain base amount, you can say, "This deal is the same for everybody. All you have to do is produce at the same level, and you will get the same compensation they are getting." Everything is transparent.

We have to remember that people talk, and as the Chinese proverb says, thinking otherwise is the same as climbing a tree with pole in hand to go fishing.

> *I have found no greater satisfaction than achieving success through honest dealing and strict adherence to the view that, for you to gain, those you deal with should gain as well.*
>
> ALAN GREENSPAN

You Take the Helm

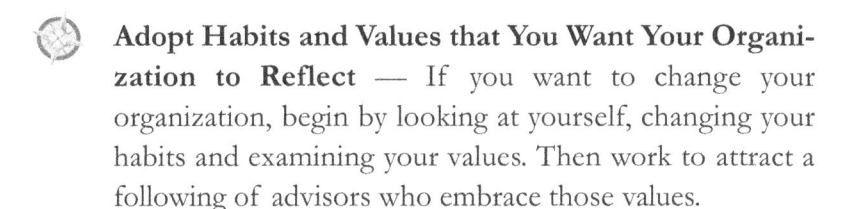

- **Adopt Habits and Values that You Want Your Organization to Reflect** — If you want to change your organization, begin by looking at yourself, changing your habits and examining your values. Then work to attract a following of advisors who embrace those values.

- **Make Your Compensation Plan Fair and Public** — Publish your compensation schedule, and be sure that everybody gets the same deal.

Chapter 17

The Universal 80-20 Rule

IN 1906, Italian economist Vilfredo Pareto created a mathematical formula to describe the unequal distribution of wealth in his country, observing that 20 percent of the people owned 80 percent of the wealth. This concept became known as the Pareto principle, or the 80-20 rule.

I first heard of the Pareto principle early in my career, when my fellow managers and I were told that 80 percent of our production would come from the top 20 percent of our advisors. Indeed, we have found that to be true over the years.

Later, I discovered that the 80-20 rule is universal; it applies at all levels of our industry. As we started looking at production numbers from other agencies, we realized that 80 percent of our company's production came from the top 20 percent of its agencies. Then, as we conducted quarterly reviews with our advisors, we saw that 80 percent of their production typically came from the top 20 percent of their client base. And with this realization came a great opportunity for us to provide value to our advisors during our quarterly reviews with them.

Spending Time at the Top

Once we realized this, we began asking them, "Are you spending 80 percent of your time with those clients?" The answer, inevitably, was "No." But each time we asked the question, we could see the lights go on in our advisors' minds. They got it. Immediately.

We can infer from the Pareto principle that if the top 20 percent of an experienced advisor's clients are so important, it makes economic sense for the advisor to spend more time in front of them. This will provide additional value to clients and will help advisors retain them because they will be devoting more time and attention to them. Furthermore, the advisors will get more and better referrals because they'll be getting them from their best clients.

Many of the advisors at North Star use a three-tiered system to prioritize their clients, as follows:

Client Category	Location on Client List
A Clients	Bottom 80 percent
AA Clients	Middle 15 percent
AAA Clients	Top 5 percent

There is an important reason that more and more of our advisors are using the designations AAA, AA and A instead of the old categories of A, B, C and D. It would be unfortunate if a lower-tier client happened to see paperwork indicating that he or she was categorized as a "D" client. Slips do happen.

Todd Bramson, one of our Top of the Table performers, originated the AAA, AA and A client-tiering concept. He thoughtfully changed the name of the game so that no client category appears unimportant. There may be unprofitable clients, but there are no unimportant clients!

Performing at the Top

Todd was a breakout speaker at MDRT (more than 1,500 people signed up for his workshop) and he is the author or co-author of several books on financial planning.[1] He spends 80 percent of his time with the top 5 percent of his clients. He mentors a new advisor who works with the next 15 percent — his AA clients. It is noteworthy that Todd is not part of the management team and is not compensated beyond splits; he mentors as a way of giving back. He subscribes to the practice that Maury Stewart believes in: "Cast your bread on the waters, and sandwiches come back."

Because Todd's junior associate brings in the AA clients, all Todd has to do is "show up." He shows up, makes a presentation to the AA client, then leaves. The junior advisor does all the proposals and spreadsheets, takes applications, arranges for physicals and makes follow-up appointments. As we mentioned in Chapter 9, the junior associate "keeps the planes in the air" by allowing Todd to spend the majority of his time working with his AAA clients. This system positions Todd as a very important, time-is-valuable professional. And he is!

As for Todd's A-level clients, they receive an annual client review letter, and his staff members — an administrative assistant and a marketing coordinator — deliver most of the service. Todd gets involved only if the situation warrants it. Most of the reviews with A clients are 15- to 20-minute phone meetings, whereas AA and AAA clients receive comprehensive reviews that last 60 to 90 minutes. If a situation arises in which A-level clients need more help,

---

[1] Todd D. Bramson, *Real-Life Financial Planning with Case Studies: An Easy-to-Understand System to Organize Your Financial Plan and Prioritize Financial Decisions*, Aspatore Books, Boston, 2006.

Thomas A. Haunty and Todd D. Bramson, *Real-Life Financial Planning for Young Lawyers: A Young Lawyers' Guide to Building the House of Their Dreams*, Aspatore Books, Boston, 2006.

David J. Johnson and Todd D. Bramson, *Real-Life Financial Planning for the High-Income Specialist: An Easy-to-Understand System to Organize Your Financial Plan and Prioritize Financial Decisions*, Aspatore Books, Boston, 2006.

Todd D. Bramson, *Real-Life Financial Planning: An Easy-to-Understand System to Organize Your Financial Plan and Prioritize Financial Decisions*, Aspatore Books, Boston, 2005.

Todd D. Bramson and Marshall W. Gifford, *Real-Life Financial Planning for the Young Dental Professional: A Dental Professional's Guide to Financial Security*, Aspatore Books, Boston, 2005.

Marshall W. Gifford and Todd D. Bramson, *Real-Life Financial Planning for the New Physician: A Resident, Fellow, and Young Physician's Guide to Financial Security*, Aspatore Books, Boston, 2005.

Todd offers to spend more time on their case and bills them at an hourly rate.

The big winners in this arrangement are Todd's clients. His AAA clients receive his undivided attention. His AA clients receive an initial presentation from him and excellent follow-up service from qualified mentees who are guided by top advisors and capable back-office team members. And his A clients receive better service from individuals who can spend more time with them. Top of the Table performers can no longer afford to spend their time working with clients at that level, regardless of how much they would like to.

Helping Advisors Get Better Client Referrals

Our experienced advisors continue to upgrade their clientele so that they have more AAA clients by obtaining quality referrals from their current clients.

One of the challenges to getting great referrals is clients' reluctance to refer "up." They seem to have no difficulty referring us to people at or below their own economic or power position. But a teacher, for example, is reluctant to refer our advisors to his physician and a physician is reluctant to refer our advisors to the head of her department. We coach advisors to deal with this phenomenon in two ways.

Getting Referrals Through Respect

The first way is with the use of the magic word "respect." Instead of just asking for names in their profile markets, our advisors learn to ask clients for the names of the people they most respect in that market. For example, if an advisor is working with a dentist, instead of just asking for referrals to other dentists, the advisor asks for information about the dentists the client most respects — dentists in town, from her graduating class or in her specialty area.

Imagine the improvement in the "set appointment" ratio when an advisor calls and says, "I've been doing some work with Dr. Smith, and during the course of our conversations, she mentioned that of all the orthodontists in New York, she respects you most."

How could someone turn down a request for a meeting after a compliment like that? Compliments are powerful.

Getting Referrals Through "Upmarketing"

The second way to improve the quality of your advisors' referrals is to have them "upmarket"; that is, focus on getting referrals only from the top 20 percent of their clients, who are likely to provide referrals whose situations are similar to or better than their own. This is precisely what happens when you coach the 80-20 rule: the more advisors focus on the top 20 percent of their clients, the better their referral pool will be. The more advisors focus on their AAA clients, the more likely they are to mentor younger advisors to provide service to AA and A clients, and to review and implement plans with those clients. The intended consequence is better service for the AA and A clients and better persistency for everyone.

So we coach our advisors to spend more and more of their precious time with the people who will benefit from their attention most and who will give them the greatest return on their time. Our Advisor of the Year in 2006, Shaun McDuffee, is also a Top of the Table qualifier and the regional vice president in our Austin, Texas, office. Shaun gave newer advisors the names of 900 engineering clients, clients he acquired when he first joined North Star in our Madison, Wisconsin, office. Shaun did this as a result of his commitment to work only with five specialties in medicine. Quite a gamble, but quite a result — last year, Shaun acquired 252 new physician clients, all jointly (because they were all split accounts, more than 500 physicians were converted to clients). All these accounts are served by newer associates and a very capable staff.

To structure their business so they can spend more time with top clients, advisors such as Shaun and Todd mentor newer advisors who are looking for people to talk to. They are not exceptions to the rule. Marshall Gifford, Dave Johnson, Anthony Williams, Marc Ortega, Eric Seybert, Joe Tocchini and Mark Bonnett are but a few of the many perennial MDRT advisors in the medical market who demonstrate every day that this approach works. Our top producers mentor newer advisors; in doing so, they set the stage to create succession plans for their own practices.

> *If we did realize the difference between the vital few and the trivial many in all aspects of our lives, and if we did something about it, we could multiply anything that we valued.*
>
> RICHARD KOCH

You Take the Helm

- **Apply the 80-20 Rule Yourself** — Devote 80 percent of your time to the top 20 percent of your advisors.

- **Encourage Your Advisors to Apply the 80-20 Rule** — Coach your advisors to assess their businesses. They will discover, inevitably, that 80 percent of their revenue is coming from 20 percent of their clients. Those are the clients they should be nurturing.

Chapter 18

Create a Mentoring Culture
Increase Revenue, Decrease Costs

MY FASCINATION with mentoring began, like many other things in my life, when I was a child in New York City. As often happens when we're young, I saw something that had a profound impact on my life that exists to this day. I saw a very large poster on a building across from our apartment on Avenue A. At the time I was attending P.S. 122, the grade school I attended from the first through third grades, so I was between five and eight years old when this happened. The poster depicted a tall, slender man leaning over to assist a very young boy in the midst of some difficulties. The caption on the poster read, "A man has never stood so tall as when he stoops to help a child." I never forgot that, and I am certain that my love for the concept of mentoring was born on that day.

Our organization is one of many around the world that successfully uses the GAMA/MDRT Joint Mentoring Program[1]. The program has been a godsend for many field leaders because of the

---

[1] For information about the GAMA/MDRT Joint Mentoring Program, call (800) 879-6378 or (847) 692-6378, or visit www.mdrt.org/benefits/mentoring.

extent to which it benefits everyone involved — mentors, mentees, the organization and the client.

An informal Web site survey conducted by NAIFA asked advisors, "Which of these helped you the most to survive your first few years in the business?" The choices were: "Had a strong mentor," "Carved out a niche," "Followed up on qualified leads," "Developed good time-management skills," "Acquired a credential" and "Built an extensive network."

Building an extensive network was at the bottom of the list, as reported in the August, 2006 issue of NAIFA's *Advisor Today* magazine. Tied for second place at 16 percent each were following up on qualified leads and carving out a niche. The hands-down winner was having a strong mentor. Fifty-two percent of respondents said their mentor was most important to them during their early years. This is an extraordinary opportunity for field leaders.

The goal of the GAMA/MDRT program is for mentees, or aspirants, to qualify for MDRT membership, and the mentors' role is to help them reach that goal.

When GAMA and MDRT introduced their joint mentoring program, there was no doubt whatsoever that we would be a part of it.

Mentors Become More Productive

As discussed in Chapter 17, mentors who work with junior advisors benefit because they are able to spend more time with their AAA clients and build their client base from better referrals. At the 2006 GAS study group meeting, we learned that the Northwestern Mutual results after three years mirrored those of New York Life and MassMutual in the increase in production of both mentors and mentees who participate in their mentoring programs.

According to statistics from the GAMA/MDRT Joint Mentoring Program, mentors increase their productivity when they begin mentoring aspirants. Once again, Maury's admonition proved timeless: "Cast your bread on the waters, and it'll come back sandwiches."

Mentees Meet Affluent Clients

Mentees who team up with senior advisors are more likely to meet affluent prospects whom they otherwise would not have had the confidence, ability or expertise to call on. Through this exposure to more affluent prospects and to the mentor's expertise, mentees are able to work on larger cases than they otherwise would, and their production and income reflect those advantages.

Organizations Increase Revenues and Decrease Costs

Organizations that cultivate a mentoring culture derive many benefits.

Increased Production for Our Advisors

First, our advisors — both the junior advisors who are mentees and MDRT aspirants and the senior advisors who are mentors — are more productive and more satisfied. Industry and blue-chip company experience confirm this.

Increased Retention of Our Advisors

Second, a formal mentoring program helps us retain advisors.

Shaun McDuffee, who is a perennial MDRT and Top of the Table qualifier in our organization, wrote an article titled "Using Mentoring to Make a Difference." Shaun's article explains the many benefits he has personally derived from the mentoring program. He said that the program has increased North Star's retention rate: "Our agency retention level started to rise dramatically during the 10 years that we formally embraced the mentoring model. Our agency is now enjoying a retention rate that is almost three times the industry average. I credit this almost entirely to the mentoring model. Our new people who are partnered with a mentor are much more likely to succeed because they know that someone cares and someone is watching. They do not want to let their mentors down."[2] It is no

---

[2] Phillip Shaun McDuffee, CLU, ChFC, "Using Mentoring to Make a Difference," *Round the Table*, May/June 2004, p. 20.

coincidence that Shaun's production in 2006 set a Securian all-time company record by a wide margin over the previous one set in 2002.

When Scott Richards, North Star's president, and Ed Deutschlander designed our new-advisor training programs, they elected to use as part of their preamble the strong advice to all new people that part of their job is to get adopted by a senior associate. During the first year, a new advisor has a senior associate who is formally charged with doing joint work with that person. The program anticipates the sophomore slump experienced by so many newer advisors, so it is an attempt to insulate them with a mentor during that vulnerable time. As you might imagine, the need to get "adopted" has some desirable by-products, not the least of which is the commendable behavior of newer advisors trying to get the attention of some of our better senior associates.

A Management Laboratory
Third, all of our MDRT-level advisors have the chance to try their hand in a training role. The mentor's role in this case is a show-and-tell role, not a management role. There is a critical difference. We require all of our line supervisors to be MDRT-level producers and, as such, to do joint field work with newer advisors. In this way, we ensure that we don't fail to identify someone who may someday successfully grow others in management. During this mentoring process, senior advisors get to discover if they enjoy developing people, and we can then begin to determine if they may have an aptitude and desire for management.

Because we hire brand-new college graduates in our system, our advisors have not yet had a chance to experience management. Once advisors qualify for Million Dollar Round Table, we encourage them to train someone else. While it is not a requirement, the overwhelming majority of them choose to do so. That's the only way they'll really know whether they may want to pursue a career in management. As we mentioned in Chapter 7, having all MDRT-level advisors train new advisors helps us make sure that we don't overlook someone who has great skills as a manager or general agent but has not had the opportunity to demonstrate them.

Fewer Trainers to Hire

Fourth, a mentoring culture saves the firm dollars that can be deployed elsewhere. We're spared the necessity of paying as much as $150,000 a year to hire a trainer to work with our new people. Using only joint field work, our mentors train our new advisors for a very modest stipend of about $250 a month per new advisor, plus split commissions. Our experience has been enlightening. The mentor has the advantage of seeing only those prospects in their profile market, without prospecting, and with little or no service responsibilities.

An experiment now in the concept phase is to reimburse the expenses of mentors who travel to offices in other cities to mentor newer advisors there. Again, this is economical. Large salaries are unnecessary because money is not necessarily the motivation of the mentor — growing others is. What the firm gains is the cross-pollination of the culture in distant offices, transference of specialties (medical, dental, pharmacy) from one office to another and additional uniformity of skills among advisors in various offices.

For example, Todd Bramson (Madison, Wisconsin) is mentoring one advisor in our Miami office and one in Portland in the medical market. Marc Ortega and Anthony Williams (Phoenix) are mentoring three advisors in our Portland office in the medical market. Ali Rizvi (Phoenix) is mentoring an advisor in the Portland office in the pharmacy market. Shaun McDuffee (Austin) is mentoring two advisors in Kansas City and one in Chicago, all in the medical market. Dave Johnson is mentoring one advisor in Cleveland and one in Indianapolis, both in the medical market. Marshall Gifford is mentoring an advisor in Chicago in the medical market.

All these situations occurred spontaneously, not as the result of a corporate strategy. Mentoring took hold and spread like wildfire because of a giving culture that cherishes helping others.

It is also noteworthy that the mentors listed above have written no less than eight books geared to the financial needs of physicians, dentists or pharmacists.

Clients Receive Superior Service

Our clients and prospects are the biggest winners. Top-tier clients receive the services of our more experienced advisors, and less affluent clients receive dedicated attention from our newer associates, who are able to rely on all of the firm's resources when the situation warrants it.

Positioning the Senior Advisor as an Expert

It is critical to remember that in this model, the mentor or trainer is not in management. Mentors do not conduct classroom training or teach presentation or closing skills. They're teachers only in terms of show and tell; that is, they make their presentation to a physician or a dentist and the new associate is there simply as an observer and student. Again, we have the medical model to thank: the system resembles that of a teaching hospital where staff physicians perform medical procedures as medical students and interns learn.

The aspirants serve as telemarketers, making all of the appointments and doing all of the prospecting and follow up. They are taught that their objective is to keep the plane in the air — in other words, to keep the experienced MDRT-level advisor in front of people.

Following is an example of what a mentee might say to a referred lead when setting up an appointment. Please keep in mind that this is not a cold call but a legitimate referred lead from a client or policyholder. Troy Korsgaden describes a similar process in more detail in his book, with the exception that Troy has an office team member, not an advisor, make the call.[3]

---

[3]Troy Korsgaden, *Power Position Your Agency: A Guide to Insurance Agency Success,* Troy Korsgaden Systems, Visalia, California, 1998, pp. 15–27.

"Hello, Ms. Reed. I'm calling for Dan Dorsey. John Jones is one of Dan's clients, and he referred Dan to you. My purpose in calling is to invite you to come in to meet Mr. Dorsey so that he can outline for you the kind of work he has done for your colleague. I'm wondering if we can do that next Tuesday at four o'clock, or would lunch on Wednesday be more convenient for you?"

The prospect might say, "Well, what is all of this about?" The junior advisor may respond with, "Ma'am, I'm afraid you're going to have to ask Mr. Dorsey about that. He has done the work with Mr. Jones. I was not part of that meeting, so I'm unable to tell you the kind of work that he did. Would Tuesday at four o'clock work for you, or would lunch on Wednesday be better?"

When the referred lead comes into the office, where all of our software, plans and backup materials are, our "Director of First Impressions" — our receptionist — greets the prospect. Then the mentee introduces himself or herself, shakes hands with the prospect and escorts the prospect to the senior advisor's office.

This process positions the senior MDRT-level advisor as an expert. Even experts couldn't position themselves as well as a mentee can frame them. Stated differently, others can sell you much better than you can sell yourself.

A Mentoring Success Story

Dan Dorsey, who is one of our advisors, actually doubled his production in only 12 months because he moved into a mentoring role with newer people. The junior associates he works with are prospecting only among Dan's profile market, which is composed of married couples from age 35 to age 50 with a dual income of $110,000 to $185,000. Dan will accept appointments only with those prospects who meet his profile, without regard to their profession. That's Dan's sweet spot. That's where he focuses, and that's where he trains his new people to focus.

This young man has doubled his production in only one year because he has started mentoring other associates. He has more appointments than he has ever had, and because his mentees make his appointments, he spends much less time prospecting.

> *The growth and development of people is the highest calling of leadership.*
>
> HARVEY FIRESTONE

You Take the Helm

- **Provide Clients with Superior Service** — Your clients will be the ultimate beneficiaries of your mentoring program. Your top-ranked clients will receive the dedicated service of your most experienced advisors, and your other clients will receive intense service of more junior but highly qualified and supported advisors who have more time to devote to them.

- **Enjoy Increased Productivity** — Establishing a mentoring program will help your organization increase skill levels and income and will decrease training costs.

- **Discover Management Talent** — Mentoring provides you with an opportunity to discover which advisors have an aptitude and passion for a mentoring role and possibly a career in management. Frank Tyger said, "One of the greatest talents of all is the talent to recognize and develop talent in others."

- **Position Junior Advisors to Succeed** — Junior advisors get to work with higher-caliber clients than they would normally meet so early in their careers, which increases their productivity and income levels.

- **Position Senior Advisors as Experts** — A mentoring culture benefits senior advisors because their mentees schedule appointments for them and position them as experts, allowing the senior advisors to spend more time with their top clients and enabling them to obtain quality referrals from them.

Chapter 19

The Power of the Many
Study Groups for Managers and Advisors

THE JOURNEY toward lifelong learning, along with the lessons it yields, has taught us that we are far more effective through the power of the many than we are individually.

Many team members in our organization benefit from frequent get-togethers such as Executive Committee gatherings, Bible study groups, advisor study groups, Toastmasters and other mutual-support gatherings.

The lesson is clear — shared ideas morph into better ideas in the light of day.

Study groups for both managers and advisors provide one of the critical requirements for success in our industry, if not life itself: accountability. So it's no surprise that many field leaders and advisors have come to depend on study groups to help them remain motivated and focused on their goals.

At a very basic level, a study group is a collection of people in similar positions with comparably sized firms who get together regularly to share best practices and hold each other accountable. But study groups can also be life-changing experiences, building a community of members who support one another in business and in personal growth. Study group members offer advice and counsel and serve as a resource to which members can turn when in need of advice. Through the power of mutual support, study groups create a capacity for growth that is bigger than any one member or firm.

Study Group Characteristics
Traditionally, study groups for field leaders involve 10 to 15 individuals who represent either one company or a range of companies. Members are from different geographical areas, but typically they represent firms of similar sizes and business models. Meetings are held annually or semiannually for two-and-a-half to three days.

The dynamics and culture of each group are, of course, different. Some groups favor more austere settings for their meetings and are strictly business; others stay at luxury resorts and invite spouses to attend, blending business with social activities. Groups differ in how much emphasis they place on sharing best practices, holding one another accountable, investigating industry trends and enhancing practice management. However, the golden threads that run through all of them are the consanguinity that develops, the best practices that are shared and the commonality of commitment to lifelong learning that characterizes the group.

Study group meetings follow a predetermined agenda and always include a report by each member (which usually highlights the firm's best practices), a discussion of the firm's accomplishments and missteps and a sharing of goals and objectives. Members are free to share any personal developments as well, and frequently they do. Some groups include outside speakers, presentations by the host firm's management team, research studies or hot-topic discussions.[1]

---

[1] *A Guide to Establishing Study Groups,* GAMA International, Falls Church, Virginia, 2006, p. 3.

The Powerful Impact of Study Groups for Field Leaders

Years ago, I was at the Phoenician Hotel in Phoenix, Arizona, for the annual meeting of a study group that I am privileged to be a part of — we call it simply "The Group" — which is one of the industry's original study groups. My fellow study group members included Charlie Smith, Maury Stewart, Al Granum, Bill Pollakov, Gary Daniels, Gary Simpson, Mike O'Malley, Joe Oakes, Brud Hodgkins, Tim Murray and Ron Lee.

During his presentation, Charlie Smith asked the group a simple question: "What are the things that have caused each of you to be successful in your career? Was it a mentor? Your company?" We each wrote out our top three influences. Number one, far and away, was the LAMP experience. That was the single greatest reason cited by the people in that group as the reason for their success. Not simply the LAMP meeting — the LAMP *experience*. For those of you who have not made this annual pilgrimage part of your routine, please note that the very best in our business have acknowledged its value.

Second on the list was study groups. That surprised a lot of people — the fact that these little meetings that take place once a year among 10 to 15 friends, all from different companies living in different cities, could have such a tremendous and profound impact on the careers of some of the most successful practitioners in America. That was an epiphany.

Later, while representing GAMA's Executive Committee at a meeting of the industry's Joint Executives Committee in Jackson Hole, Wyoming, I brought up the fact that this incredible opportunity was available to only a few general agents and managers. At that time, there were 15 members of The Group, 20 members of the Research Agency Group (RAG) and 10 members of the General Agents Symposium (GAS) group — a total of 45 study group members. But eight of us were in more than one group, so really only 37 people in America were benefiting from these powerful study groups that were credited with being the No. 2 reason for the success of some of the top-performing leaders in our industry.

So in 2004, with help from Ed Deutschlander, I became actively engaged in executing this "power of the many" initiative throughout our industry by forming five GAMA International study groups for field leaders with the help of Bob Savage, Ron Lee, John Langdon, Harry Hoopis, Wayne Swenson and John Baier. The groundswell reaction was so overwhelming that I can recall only one invitation that was not accepted, and that individual is no longer in our industry. The pent-up demand by all others was simply tremendous.

While the original intent was to form three new study groups, the positive reaction of the leaders in our industry was so intense that we had to increase the number of intercompany groups to five. This raised the number of field leaders involved in this powerful resource from 37 to more than 100, and the demand for such groups continues to surge. GAMA has embraced this movement, is taking it to the next level and stands ready to assist others who are interested in its benefits.

Your Personal Board of Directors

I think most field leaders would add to their wish list the luxury of having their own personal board of directors. That's just what a study group is. A study group gives you access to the best and most expensive talent in America. You get to meet with them at least annually and run problems up the flagpole to get their opinions, ideas, experience and wisdom to help you solve problems and come up with creative ways for you to build your firm and sustain that growth.

The dedicated, hard-working members of study groups share the details of their successes as well as lessons they learned from things that didn't go so well. As a study group member, you share your goals with that group of people. You also benefit from their feedback in terms of what you're doing right and what you could be doing better.

Study groups serve as an accountability mechanism because they encourage members to share with the group what their firm or agency performance will be in the next year in terms of their metrics, including the number of cases, the amount of premium, revenue, insurance in force, persistency, advisor retention and number of recruits. It's a living process. When you return the next year, your presentation should include the goals you shared a year earlier, comparing those with what your actual results were.

Field leaders who are not involved in a study group are missing this highly effective business and personal accountability mechanism. Some are either accountable to their home office or, in many cases, to no one other than themselves. Accountability works for our advisors using our quarterly review meetings, and study groups serve the same purpose for us.

A Group of Trusted Confidants

A professional study group also provides a great deal of consanguinity — a connection with a core group of people from different companies that's so close that you are able to say anything you want without consequence or reprisal. This is a challenge in an *intra*-company study group meeting because things you say have a way of getting out. But in an *inter*company study group, everything that goes on is confidential, unless a fellow study group member releases you from that confidentiality.

Members of study groups automatically develop close friendships, and friends dislike letting other friends down. That dynamic provides a further incentive to do what you say you are going to do, as well as to maintain confidences, which are characteristics of any good friendship.

Populating Study Groups

When study groups were originally founded, the typical policy was that no two people from the same city or from the same company were allowed to be in the same study group. For example, when Bill Pollakov was going through the chairs leading to the GAMA presidency, he changed companies a year or two before his term as president and subsequently joined MassMutual. We already had a general agent from MassMutual in our GAS Group, so Bill — the future president of GAMA — was expected to step aside from our study group. (To this day, he is still not in the group because it has another member who is a MassMutual general agent.) Bill understood the reasons and, being the gentleman that he is, automatically resigned. As you might imagine, it was not one of our happier days.

Since that time, the decrease in the number of firms in America means that there is less competition among them and more of a willingness to let people from the same cities, and even from the same companies, into the same study group.

John Langdon, who was in the GAS Group with me, was compelled to find a new company when his previous company abandoned face-to-face distribution. John and his partner, Steve Ford, found themselves without a company. They finally elected to join my company, Securian. My fellow GAS Group members — including Bob Savage, Harry Hoopis, Nick Horn, John Baier, Luis Chiappy, Ron Long and Ron Lee — then discussed this fact and said, "The rule is that he's out of the group unless you want a different result." I'm happy to report that John is still part of the GAS Group.

But if two members from the same company are uncomfortable with the situation, then alternatives need to be considered.

Realizing the Powerful Impact of Study Groups for Advisors

Study groups help advisors excel in building their practices and accumulating quality clients.

Study group meetings for advisors are known by many different names, including sales builder or career builder groups and advisor study groups, but they serve essentially the same purposes. Also, as a general rule, after advisors attain Million Dollar Round Table status, they are eligible to join MDRT-sponsored study groups.

Whereas most field-leader study groups are formed by individuals, most advisor study groups are formed by firm management and are therefore made up of advisors who all work for the same organization. The prototype for this kind of support group was developed by Management Hall of Famer Bill Cochran of

Northwestern Mutual, who formalized the process in his agency in Nashville and later gave the system to GAMA International for use by the industry. Today it serves as the benchmark against which others are compared.

Like study groups for field leaders, advisor study groups also require members to share their progress for the previous time period and to set goals for the next time period. But advisors usually meet much more often than field leaders do — typically once a week for newer advisors and once a month for more experienced advisors.

In these meetings, advisors in our firm stand before the group at a blackboard or flipchart and write down their "vital metrics" for the previous week, as well as their goals or objectives for the next week. These numbers include sales made, sales pending, calls made, forward appointments on the books and referred leads obtained — all of the metrics that advisors need to be accountable for. They are, in essence, putting their commitments in the public domain to achieve certain performance goals during the next time period.

Advisor groups typically have fewer members than field leaders' study groups — usually four to 10. Sometimes a supervisor or manager attends the meetings. The real power of advisor groups is creating advisors' accountability to one another, the knowledge that on each Monday or Friday morning — whenever their group meets — they are going to have to report publicly to their peers about their performance, behavior and history over the last seven days. It's a very powerful tool.

These accountability meetings bring the advisors' competitive nature to the forefront. They want to be the best among all others in the group. They want to get more referred leads than the next person, more appointments on their books, more premiums or more cases. That friendly competitiveness is very much a motivator and a driver in the advisor groups. Just as important are the case studies and best practices that they share.

Being involved in study groups helps us grow as people and as professionals. And providing our advisors with an opportunity to grow and reach their potential through accountability meetings helps us fulfill our role as servant leaders.

> *Good men prefer to be accountable.*
> MICHAEL EDWARDES

You Take the Helm

- **Hold Yourself Accountable** — Consider joining or forming an industry study group so you will have a trusted group of peers — a personal board of directors — to challenge you, to offer alternative strategies and to support your personal and professional growth.

- **Create Peer Accountability for Your Advisors** — Establish advisor study groups so that advisors can hold one another accountable for meeting their goals. GAMA International can help.

- **Build Professional Relationships** — Study groups provide friendships in what otherwise may be a lonely business at the top. Joseph Addison said, "Friendship improves happiness and abates misery, by doubling our joy and dividing our grief."

Chapter 20

Coach, Don't Coax

IN 1968, when I was a home office employee with Minnesota Mutual, we had an attorney named Ken Deason who also worked in the Agency Department. Ken's favorite saying (we heard it from him frequently) was, "You can't shine crap." (He used a more colorful alliteration, but we've cleaned it up for the book!) Whenever we had advisors who were failing and their managers or general agents had worked with them extensively but to no effect, Ken would stoically repeat this comment.

The more I thought about it, the more I realized it was true. You can't do something with nothing. In fact, many of us in the department began using that phrase among ourselves (usually when members of the gentler sex were not present). Later, women, too, began using it as a shortcut to clear communication and understanding.

For many years, I followed that principle and shared it with others when appropriate — including friends who weren't in our industry.

A New Twist on an Old Saying

As a child growing up in Manhattan, my best friend was Richard Pastorella. He later became a member of the New York City Police Department's bomb squad. Richie and I maintained our relationship for many years following my move away from New York City. Later Richie became a predental student at New York University during the day while working his way through school by walking a beat as an NYPD policeman in Brooklyn at night. He liked police work so much that he eventually abandoned his dream of becoming a dentist and instead dedicated himself to full-time police work. He was quickly promoted to sergeant and later to lieutenant. They next asked him to work on the bomb squad. Being one of the most daring ringaliveo contestants on Lower East Side rooftops as a child, he was unable to refuse the assignment.

On the night of December 31, 1981, Richie was working when the Puerto Rican terrorist group FALN planted a bomb at the Lower Manhattan Federal Courthouse building. Richie arrived on the scene to disarm the bomb. As he reached his hands into the box, he set off the trigger for a second bomb. Clearly, the device was intended to kill as well as destroy property. The subsequent explosion blew Richie horizontally more than a hundred feet through the air. One of his colleagues, dog handler Tony Senft, was with his dog 40 feet behind Richie and lost an eye as a result of that explosion. Both of Richie's eyeballs disintegrated, he lost all five fingers on his right hand, and he lost all hearing in one ear and 95 percent of his hearing in the other ear. The fact that he did not die that New Year's Eve was nothing short of divine intervention. He was in a New York hospital for four months and received personal phone calls from President Ronald Reagan. Richie was rightly hailed as a hero.

Out of that tragedy and loss emerged a lifetime of purpose for Richie, as well as inspiration to everyone who knew the story. He devoted his life to traveling North America, speaking to police and firefighting organizations about rebuilding the lives of devastated families when members were killed in the line of duty. He became known nationally and has been cited for many awards. He went on to earn a master's degree in police work with the aid of a remarkable machine that turns the pages of a book as it reads to him. The fact that both of Richie's sons are NYPD policemen today is part of his legacy.

Richie and his family once visited my Phoenix home and stayed with us. When they arrived, Richie handed me a small pen holder that contained a gold pen and had a shiny little rock as its base. He said, "Phil, I got this for you. I think it's an amazing piece. Do you know what it is?"

I said, "Yeah, it looks like a piece of marble."

"It's not marble," he said. I started to turn the rock upside down to see if anything was written on the bottom, and Richie's catlike instincts told him that that's exactly what I was doing.

"Don't turn it over," Richie said. "It says what it is on the bottom."

I said, "Well, what is it? Granite?"

"No," he said. "It's not granite."

I said, "Rich, I give up. What is it?"

"It's coprolite," he answered.

"Coprolite? What is coprolite?"

"It's dinosaur sh--," he replied. "It's a billion years old."

I broke up laughing. It immediately hit me that this little rock in my hand suddenly proved wrong a tenet that I had abided by for so many years. As it turns out, you *can* shine crap — if you have a billion years to do it!

But as managers, we don't have a billion years. We have to start out with quality candidates who already have the character, attitude, skills and commitment to make it in this career.

It Begins with Selection

You can't do something with nothing. You have to start with quality managers to recruit quality advisors. "A" managers generally recruit "A"-level advisors, and "B" managers usually recruit "C"-level advisors (on a scale of A to D). Recruiting C-level advisors is self-defeating. We'd get better results throwing flower seeds on asphalt.

If you start with C-level advisors, you're going to end up coaxing them. Trying to get that flywheel in motion from a dead stop is a waste of your time. But if you start with A-level advisors, they already have within them the determination and drive to succeed, so you can coach them to success. You can use your firm's momentum to help them get to where they need to be.

I've said it many times before: "The race does not always go to the fleet of foot, strong of body or tough of mind. But that's the way to bet it." The A-level advisors are the ones you want to bet on to succeed in this business. These people don't need to be dragged, only guided.

Good managers know the difference between *coaxing* someone who isn't determined to succeed and *coaching* someone who truly wants success. When we *coax* people, we have to cajole and repeat, constantly reminding them of their goals, deliverables and obligations. But when we *coach* A-level advisors, all we're really doing is channeling their talents rather than pushing or pulling them. They propel themselves, and we do little more than guide them.

Remember that for the first 90 days, advisors will do whatever you tell them to do and will do very little of what you tell them after that. So you have a 90-day window of opportunity in which to coach them about their activities and forming the right habits.

It all begins with good selection. A rule of thumb that we use is that you will find one quality advisor in 20 candidates. But if candidates are referred by your own advisors, you can cut that 20 in half. Over the years, we've found that 10 advisor referrals from within our organization produces one hire. The tremendous take-away here is that incentives of every type should be devoted to improving this referral source. Our very own people know the culture of the organization and the degree of difficulty involved in succeeding in this career. You might expect that retention of this group of appointments would be superior to the rest, and you'd be right.

You can coach advisors only if they are truly committed to succeeding in this industry. This is a tough business, and only two of 100 people can make it. Advisors have to be just as committed to our business and its inherent rejection as medical students are to four years of medical school and three to five years of a residency program, many of them knowing that the first time they'll earn any real money is when they're almost 35 years old. It is not unusual for new physicians to begin making $160,000 at about 30 and carry $120,000 of school debt into their practices. As managers, we need to be able to identify and select those people who are committed to succeeding in this career in much the same way that medical schools identify and select their applicants. Neither profession is easy. Both require sacrifices.

Once our advisors are on board, we have to encourage them. Commissions and fees are what advisors live *on*. Serving others and receiving recognition, appreciation and encouragement are what they live *for* — especially in those first 90 to 180 days. Complimenting your advisors — providing them with verbal sunshine — is the best way to encourage good behavior. Encouragement is the oxygen that keeps the soul healthy.

When Faith Turns to Hope, the End Is Near

When we have capable, competent, quality advisors who are committed to succeeding, we have faith in the inevitability of their success. There is a longstanding admonition in our industry that when a manager's faith in advisors turns to hope, fire them. In other words, if we find ourselves hoping that advisors will succeed, as opposed to having faith that they will succeed, it is not going to work. We need to bring finality to the situation by terminating the advisor or establishing requirements that will do it automatically.

We can't hope that someone will succeed. We have to have faith that they will succeed. They, too, have to have faith that they will succeed. And they have to want to succeed more than we want them to succeed.

When we care more than the advisor does about his or her success, it is a sign that our faith in that person has turned to hope, and the end is near.

> *You can make bad wine from good grapes, but you can't make good wine from bad grapes.*
>
> PAT SMITH, DOMAIN CHARDONNE WINERIES

You Take the Helm

- **Start with Quality** — You can't do something with nothing. Select quality managers who will select quality candidates who are committed to succeeding.

- **Coach, Don't Coax** — You can coach and guide quality candidates to success. You cannot coach or coax C-level candidates to success.

- **Recognize When Faith Turns to Hope** — If you find yourself *hoping* that advisors will succeed instead of *having faith* that they will succeed, terminate them or try to recycle them — for their own good and for the good of your organization and the rest of your people, who rely on you to maintain the quality of the firm.

- **Do the Right Thing** — Kind management is sometimes cruel management. Retaining those who should be elsewhere is never benevolent. We owe them more.

Chapter 21

A High-Performance, No-Excuse Culture

ONE OF THE many reasons that the job of the financial advisor is among the most sought-after careers in the nation is the freedom that the unstructured environment allows. But unless the advisor is extremely disciplined, success is improbable. The opportunity for distraction, the office without walls and the absence of a time clock all contribute to the already difficult challenge presented by this rejection-filled career. In Chapter 4, we discussed the discipline and accountability that new advisors need from management to make it through their first 90 days in the career.

To increase the odds of successfully getting advisors beyond their first year in this business, we must establish metrics that track their activity, results and overall performance. To the extent that field management does this, our odds of growing successful advisors increase, along with our advisor retention rate.

That is why we established a high-performance culture in the early 1990s — to give advisors a better chance of making it through that tough first year. It worked well, but not well enough. We achieved a 25 percent four-year retention rate and remained there. Although this retention rate was about twice the industry average, it was unacceptable to our business model. So we explored ways to improve it.

We brainstormed the challenge in our Corporate Development Council meetings. In the no-holds-barred format of those meetings, people continued to throw out ideas. We discussed many possible strategies and concepts, but nothing was powerful enough to really make a difference. Then, somebody suggested the idea of a "no-excuse" culture. We probably thought of no fewer than 50 different ideas before someone came up with adding the no-excuse aspect to our high-performance culture.

It's a high-performance culture, and there are no excuses for poor performance. Unforeseen distractions, no matter how sad, can and must be anticipated. When used as a reason for nonperformance, they are an excuse. Advisors must be taught to anticipate that bad things do happen, and they must still validate their contract in spite of those unfortunate circumstances. As managers, we must educate advisors about this expectation and be prepared to let advisors go if they don't meet our standards. Requests for extensions on deadlines are generally the result of putting off until the last minute the fulfillment of the requirement. If this procrastination characteristic carries over to client service, there will be consequences from a compliance vantage point, so we cannot allow that to happen. Further, our "client comes first" mantra loses its force.

It was not until we added the no-excuse aspect to the equation that we began to notice significant differences. Previously, many of our newer advisors were barely validating their contracts, and we were accepting their excuses for poor performance. But once we adopted the no-excuse culture, many of our advisors were not only validating their contracts, they were max-validating them. Max-validation means that they were achieving the highest ranges of performance in the three-year subsidy program that Securian provides to new advisors at the beginning of their careers. Furthermore, almost a fifth of them were max-validating their contracts in every one of their 12 quarterly checkpoint periods over a three-year period. This was a remarkable transformation. Before we adopted the no-excuse culture, it was a rare occurrence for a new advisor to max-validate.

We have had similar experiences over the years with Securian and its part-time production requirements. Each time an old friend failed to meet the minimum production requirements and had to be terminated, there was both despair regarding the loss and genuine concern about the cumulative impact of this process on the overall future production of the firm. This latter concern has proved to be misplaced. The raising of the bar almost always causes those who remain to take the minimum levels seriously and to improve their performance. It has clearly helped them.

The number of new people who failed began to plummet, and a sense of eliteness began to emerge among those who were able to rise to the higher standards that we were setting. They felt like the few and the proud. The winning environment grew and began to feed on itself. What in the world had happened?

Why the No-Excuse Concept Works

Because of the enormous freedom inherent in an advisor's career, there were simply too many ways for us to rationalize mediocrity. In our familial environment, where family and personal obligations matter greatly, it was easy to explain away advisors who did not fulfill requirements because of what could be considered higher priorities. This proved to be a conundrum until we added the no-excuse component to the equation. When we did that, we essentially blended advisors' family and personal obligations with their commitment to this career. Meeting both types of obligations became table stakes. We expect our advisors to fulfill their career obligations within the realm of their personal obligations without using the latter as excuses for falling short on the former.

Placing obstacles in front of winners doesn't produce excuses; it defines who the winners are. Winners aren't necessarily the ones who win every time; they're the ones who never give up, who keep trying no matter what the odds are. Losers are potential winners who gave up. As Ernest Hemingway told his son, "You know what makes a good loser? Practice." Successful people are those who never stop trying, whether they're company CEOs, teachers, bread-truck drivers, physicians or ditch diggers. As long as they keep trying, without regard to monetary markers, they're winners.

So we married the no-excuse expectation to the high-performance expectation to create a sense of camaraderie, an eliteness, a gathering of eagles, a line of freight trains that plows through obstacles without excuses or rationalizations. Whether you're in a spelling bee or a bar fight, these are the people you want on your team. And that's exactly the kind of performance and can-do attitude that you'll get if you exemplify that same behavior as a manager. That's the culture that wins wars of any kind.

Turn a Spotlight on Your Culture

In his book *The People Principle: A Revolutionary Redefinition of Leadership*, Ron Willingham said, "People soon discover the level of performance that their managers will settle for and gravitate to that level."[1] As managers, we need to raise our standards, look carefully to see where excuses are endemic, and put processes in place so that underperformance is not accepted.

Underperformance comes in many different forms. Dr. Paul Stoltz categorizes underperformers as campers or quitters in his book *Adversity Quotient* and compares them with their successful counterparts — climbers.

Stoltz explains that *quitters* do just enough to get by. They demonstrate little ambition, minimal drive and sub-par quality. They take few risks and are rarely creative, except when it comes to avoiding big challenges. Quitters are the dead weight of any organization. In contrast, *campers* show some initiative and drive and put forth some effort. They will work hard on anything that helps them better

---

[1] Ron Willingham, *The People Principle: A Revolutionary Redefinition of Leadership*, St. Martin's Griffin, 1997, p.68.

secure what they already have. But they do only what is required. It is this baseline of satisfactory performance that keeps campers employed, and it frustrates the visionaries who are striving to create ultimate performance.[2]

Climbers are the people we want on our team. They embrace challenges and live with a sense of urgency. They are self-motivated and highly driven, and they strive to get the utmost out of life. They are catalysts for action and tend to make things happen. They will not settle for a career at base camp, but instead continue the climb to the top. Climbers do not settle for title or position alone. They constantly seek new ways to grow and contribute.[3]

We've had our share of quitters and campers, and we found two areas in particular where we were making excuses for people who were not performing in accordance with our standards. Once we realized our errors, we corrected them and put processes in place so that they wouldn't happen again.

Many of our advisors come through internship programs with universities throughout our 10-state area. One big mistake we had been making was that we were hiring interns and then saying, "If we like them, we'll give them our selection test later." Well, by the time we got around to testing them two summers later, some of them would fail the test, but by that time we were in love with them. We would make excuses for why the test results did not apply, and we would hire them anyway. We basically threw out our selection test, and that was not wise.

Today, before these young people even become interns, they must pass our selection test. We want to make sure that if we ever make them an offer, or if they ever want to become an advisor, that they have already taken and passed the selection test. Once you fall in love with them, it's too hard not to give them an opportunity.

---

[2]Paul G. Stoltz, Ph.D., *Adversity Quotient: Turning Obstacles into Opportunities,* Wiley, 1999, p. 19.
[3]Stoltz, p. 20.

A second big mistake we had been making was that we would hire young people after their internship and then ask them to pass the licensing tests that they need to become advisors. We paid their salaries and covered their overhead. They naturally thought that their job was to pass these licensing tests instead of getting on the phone. We finally realized that we couldn't do that anymore because no matter what we said to them, they still believed that their job was to pass the tests. Now we simply say, "The tests are table stakes. To get into the game — to get a contract — you have to pass all of your licensing tests first." Problem solved.

Today, candidates enter a pre-contract training period only after they pass all of the required licensing tests (e.g., Series 7, Series 63, life, accident), and even then they're still not on our payroll. Candidates who graduate from college on June 1, for example, would not start employment with us until September 1. During that summer, we will pay for all the tests that they have to take to become advisors, and they must pass their tests by September 1. If they don't pass, the contract remains in suspension until they do.

Scrutinizing our process in this manner helps us execute our high-performance, no-excuse culture, and we're always looking for new ideas to further improve and refine our processes.

> *There's a difference between interest and commitment. When you're interested in doing something, you do it only when circumstances permit. When you're committed to something, you accept no excuses, only results.*
>
> Art Turock

You Take the Helm

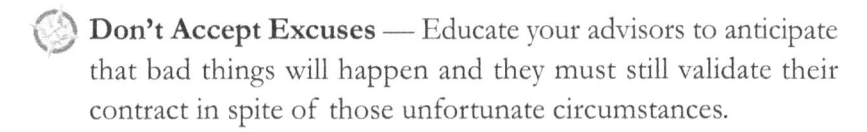

- **Don't Accept Excuses** — Educate your advisors to anticipate that bad things will happen and they must still validate their contract in spite of those unfortunate circumstances.

- **Don't Make Excuses** — No matter how sympathetic you may be to your advisors' situations or how much you like them, don't allow yourself to make excuses for their poor performance.

- **Inspect Your Systems and Processes** — Look for areas where standards are not being met and determine why. Change your processes to support your no-excuse culture.

- **Seek Out the Climbers** — Quitters give up and return to the base of the mountain, and campers find base camp and level off. Climbers want nothing less than the very top of the mountain.

- **Set High Expectations** — People will live up to your expectations, so set them high. Sustainable high performance is never accidental.

Chapter 22

Quarterly Reviews

A TREMENDOUS amount of freedom is inherent in the careers of our advisors. They expect us to add structure and accountability to the position to help them keep that freedom from becoming a liability. Quarterly reviews allow us to do just that.

The quarterly review is an extremely effective tool that I borrowed from Richard McCloskey, another Management Hall of Fame inductee. Dick has been a Master Agency Award qualifier every year since its inception, and he has used quarterly reviews effectively for many years. We've adapted Dick's process to fit into our own culture and organization.

Every publicly traded company in America is familiar with the quarterly review because every 90 days or so Wall Street analysts evaluate their performance. The analysts compare the company's quarterly results with what it said it was going to do and predict where earnings and performance will be in the future. So virtually every CEO in a publicly traded company is subject to the rigors of quarterly reviews. If this process is effective for the CEOs of huge corporations, our advisors can certainly use it to help them set and reach goals.

Reviewing our advisors' performance on a quarterly basis instead of an annual basis coincides perfectly with North Star's quarterly finish lines and checkpoints, which we discussed in Chapter 8.

At North Star, senior management conducts a quarterly performance review with individual advisors. We have 150 full-time advisors, and each review is about 20 minutes long. If you do the math, you'll see that it adds up to about 50 hours of pretty intense work every quarter. North Star's president — my son Scott — conducts the reviews in April and October, and I conduct them in January and July. The way we conduct the reviews varies slightly because of our style differences. We've learned that it's best if we take notes so that we have each other's notes in each advisor's folder.

Conducting Quarterly Reviews

Our assistant schedules a review for every half hour, allowing a 20-minute time slot for each advisor. This gives us time during the day to catch up on emails and phone calls without interrupting the reviews. Of course, we turn off our cell phones and computers during the reviews.

The review starts with one or two personal questions to break the ice.

If, during the interview, I see that something serious is going on with an advisor — truant kids, financial difficulties, a divorce, a parent with cancer — I say, "Let me offer this. Let's address the business parts of this conversation in the next few minutes, and then let's schedule a meeting for the end of the day, when it's convenient for you, when we don't have any time constraints, so we can discuss this very important matter at length." I postpone the personal discussion for a time when we're both in a more relaxed frame of mind. You don't want to shortchange someone who needs to discuss a serious issue.

The Quarterly Review Questionnaire

We use a structured form for the quarterly review (see the Appendix for a sample of the form). This questionnaire addresses our advisors' annual goals in many different areas: professional designations, life commissions and company and firm credits. Advisors could be striving for individual awards such as Advisor of the Year or Rookie of the Year. They could be trying to set various records, such as "the highest production for a female advisor in the history of the company." So the starting point of the review is to look at the individual advisor's bogeys, targets and goals as recorded in his or her annual plan.

At the top of the quarterly review questionnaire is the advisor's name, review date and the year he or she started in the business. This gives us some perspective about where each one should be at any given time. When you're dealing with as many as 150 advisors, it's not always easy to remember the year each started in the business. As you grow your firm, systems like this one can be a great help.

One Key Goal

One of the questions at the top of the sheet is, "What is your key goal this year?" Advisors can have 20 goals, but we want them to focus on one key goal — the one goal that, if they achieve it this year, no matter what else happens in every other arena, the year will be a success.

It is always a quantitative goal, but it may not have a quantitative name. For example, Million Dollar Round Table doesn't have a quantitative name, but the goal is quantitative. The requirement changes annually; in any given year, advisors know the exact amount of first-year commissions they need to qualify. As we've said elsewhere, if you can measure it, you can manage it. If you can't measure it, you can't manage it.

The Critical Number

The second question is, "What is your critical number?" That number will be different for each advisor. As we discussed in Chapter 8, the critical number is the one number you fight for and have confidence in; if you make that critical number, your other goals will most likely fall into place.

The critical number is not the same as the annual goal. Annual MDRT qualification cannot be a critical number because a critical number must be much shorter in duration — usually daily or, later, weekly. The most common critical number for our advisors, especially new ones, is to have 30 appointments with prospective clients written in their appointment books at all times. This number lets everyone know whether they've won or lost today.

At Penn Mutual, Maury Stewart had a critical number of two prepaid applications per week. This would ensure 100 paid cases in a year. Maury said, "If you do 100 lives a year, everything else will take care of itself." In my entire career, I have yet to see an advisor fail in this business after hitting that target.

Expose the Insanity of Wishful Thinking

The next two questions are about the advisor's key annual goal: "Are you ahead, or are you behind?" and "By how much?" We want to quantify where they are and what they need to do. If an advisor is significantly behind where he needs to be at this point to reach his annual goal, we come to a critical part of the interview. It is apparent to both of us that the advisor will not be able to hit the goal in the next 30 days. So we ask, "Do you want to reduce your goal?" Most advisors say no, so the next question is, "What are you going to do to change the result you've been getting?" In other words, the advisor has to either change his goal or change his activity level.

As the old saying goes, the definition of insanity is doing the same thing over and over again and expecting a different result. If the advisor does not want to lower his goal or change his expectations, he can't continue to behave as he has in the past because that behavior put him behind in reaching the goal. If he's halfway through the year and only a quarter of the way to his goal, he's going to have to triple his activity to catch up and hit the goal. If he's not prepared to do that, then we must lower the goal. This is an important point that allows field leaders to add value by exposing the insanity of wishful thinking.

So far, we've been looking at the goal from an annual perspective. We transition to a quarterly time frame with the following question: "What did you say you would do in the last 90 days, and what, in fact, have you done during that period?" There will be one of two outcomes: Either the advisor has done what he said he would do (or more) or he has not done what he said he was going to do. If he has missed his quarterly goal, the next question is, "Why?"

We are trying to get advisors to look candidly and honestly at their performance, measure that performance and think critically about it. It's human nature when we haven't achieved what we set out to achieve to try not to think about it — to look for a foxhole or go into denial. The objective in the review is to bring the data into the open and light up the foxhole.

If an advisor doesn't hit his quarterly goal, chances are he's going to be behind on his annual goal. If that's the case, we have to lower the annual goal or the advisor must commit to a different activity level from the one that caused him to miss his quarterly goal.

Sometimes the choice is clear. For example, an advisor whose goal was $100,000 of first-year commissions or 100 cases this year could lower that goal without any repercussions. But if an advisor is in his fifth year and his goal is to qualify for Million Dollar Round Table, he cannot lower that goal. He must raise his activity level to meet the goal because advisors in their fifth year or beyond must qualify for MDRT to stay with our organization. In return for the deliverables that our firm has committed to providing to our advisors (including quarterly reviews), they commit to qualifying for MDRT.

Simply defining your minimum acceptable level of performance establishes your game plan.

The Big "Why"

The next question is, "What is your motivation to hit your goal?" Our axiom is, "If you have a big enough *why*, you'll figure out the *what* and the *how*." That's what we're trying to get at here with this question: "What gets you out of bed in the morning and off to work to achieve something?" Advisors have a passion for the "why" that will motivate them to hit their goals. It could be, "I want to lead the organization," "I want to put my sister through college" or "I want to buy my parents a home." If they have a big enough why, they'll figure out how to do it. Ali Rizvi wanted to put his sister through undergraduate and graduate school; he did it and is now paying for another sister's medical school in Pakistan. Dan Willy wanted to buy a house for his parents, who had never lived in one. Those are big whys. Smart leaders wouldn't bet against Ali or Dan. That's what we're looking for.

Personal Income
Next, we shift to income. This is really a gut check: "What was your income last year?" And the next question is critical: "Were you satisfied with that income?" If they say yes, that's a good thing. But that's not the normal response. The normal response is, "No, I'm not satisfied with it." Why is that the typical answer? Because advisors are hunters, not gatherers. They eat what they kill, and thank God for that. It doesn't matter, quantitatively, what their income was. They seldom find complete contentment in what has happened; they're always striving to be better, to achieve more. That's what makes them great advisors. They're "goal-seeking animals," a term Aristotle used. They love goals, and they continue to increase those goals. They convert dreams to goals by putting deadlines on them. Field leaders should strive to be the catalyst in this process.

Income is in the advisor's control, so we ask, "What do you want your income to be this year?" The next question is even more important: "Why do you want that amount?" Again, we're getting not to my motivation or the firm's motivation, but to the advisor's motivation to hit his or her personal goal.

Life Production
Next we look at the advisor's life production goal for last year and ask, "What will it be this year?" Because our firm is a life-based

financial planning organization, we believe that the person who controls the life insurance sale controls the relationship. It's not a coincidence that our leading life producers — such as our Top of the Table producers Jeff Jarnes and Mike Brocker — are also among our top five securities producers. Their client relationships are built on trust, which they developed through the life sales process.

We ask our advisors if they are ahead or behind on their life production goal, and by how much. We drill down on this goal to see where they are on an annual basis.

The final question about income is, "What are you going to do differently to increase your income to a level where you will be satisfied?" We want to end this part of the discussion talking about activity: "What are you going to do to improve your results?"

To change their results, advisors must change their activity. Al Granum figured it all out for us 40 years ago with his 10-3-1 One Card System. Ten quality referrals gets us three prospects, resulting in one client. Assuming that our advisors keep good records, we can work with them to review their activity over the past month, quarter and year and make the necessary upward adjustments.

Michael Gerber discusses this concept in *The E Myth Revisited*. He calls it "information systems" and lists the following benchmarks:

- How many calls were made?
- How many prospects were reached?
- How many appointments were scheduled?
- How many appointments were confirmed?
- How many appointments were held?
- How many needs-analysis presentations were scheduled, confirmed and completed?
- How many solutions presentations were scheduled, confirmed and completed?
- What was the average dollar amount?

Gerber says this exercise will tell you which of your advisors are using your selling system and which are not. It will tell you what needs to be changed.[1]

Lifelong Learning

The quarterly review moves on to "What tests have you taken and passed in the past 90 days?" We're talking about professional designations. From an educational point of view, we're always interested in the progress our advisors are making on earning the CLU, ChFC and CFP. This is a profession, and the litmus test of one's devotion to it is commitment to obtaining these designations. Our clients deserve nothing less.

To the greatest extent possible, we want our advisors to focus on the CLU and ChFC designations, with subsequent attention to the CFP. We are a life-driven organization, and we want to control client relationships. The CLU helps us do that better than any other single designation. The ChFC stresses business rather than individual solutions and is a great fit for our markets.

The overwhelming majority of people I've known in my career who started with the CFP designation have not gone on to achieve the CLU and ChFC designations. But many of those who earn the CLU or ChFC designations do go on to achieve the CFP. I earned the CLU 20 years before I attained the CFP. I believe in both, but my experience compels me to encourage advisors to enroll in The American College programs (CLU and ChFC) first.

Of course, from a professional point of view, we would like our people to have all three designations. We want people who are committed to a lifetime of learning, and there are ample opportunities for that in our industry. No one can learn everything about financial planning in one lifetime. There's just too much information to master, and it's growing exponentially. And let's not forget that clients want specialists, not generalists, in this complex environment.

---

[1]Michael E. Gerber, *The E Myth Revisited: Why Most Small Businesses Don't Work and What to Do About It,* HarperCollins Publishers, New York, 2001, pp. 247–248.

Contests, Challenges and Solutions

After the educational piece, we come back to company and firm contests, including Securian's national convention, international convention and Chairman's Club meetings, as well as North Star's meetings and conventions. We ask, "Where are you in terms of those milestones?"

Next, we say, "Tell me what the three greatest challenges in your business are." We don't care about the order. We write them down and say, "Tell me what you're going to do about each one." We love to hear advisors talk about themselves and their goals. It gives us special insight into the inner person we're trying to coach.

From there, we go to a series of three questions and three possible solutions. This section of the quarterly review is focused on how North Star can help the advisor grow as an individual.

The three questions are:

- "What goals are you putting off?"
- "What will you have accomplished before the end of the next quarter?"
- "What is your plan to increase administrative and marketing support?"

We continuously try to convince advisors to delegate the $20-an-hour work and focus on the $400- an-hour work — namely, being in front of people. As stated elsewhere, we want to keep the planes in the air, not on the tarmac.

Finally, we ask our advisors how North Star can help them achieve their goals, how they want us to hold them accountable so they can meet their goals and what the firm is or is not doing to help them. With newer advisors, we sometimes ask, "If you were CEO of this firm, what would you do, stop doing or do differently?" Fresh ideas provide us with new building blocks.

As you can see, our quarterly reviews aim for in-depth insight into each advisor's mindset, motivation and progress. These reviews provide a systematic way to hold advisors accountable for their performance and keep them on track to meet their goals. They ensure that we connect with the advisors regularly and find out what's going on in their professional and personal lives.

> *I think it is an immutable law in business that words are words, explanations are explanations, promises are promises — but only performance is reality.*
>
> HAROLD S. GENEEN

You Take the Helm

- **Hold Your Advisors Accountable** — Review critical performance data for your advisors on a quarterly basis. This allows you to hold them accountable for their performance, help them stay on track to meet their goals and build your professional relationship with them.

- **Discover the Big "Why"** — Understand each advisor's passion and commitment to his or her goals.

- **Require Results** — Advisors who are not on track to meet their goal must lower that goal or increase their activity to get back on track.

- **Exchange Deliverables** — Require minimum production levels in return for the value your firm delivers to your advisors.

- **Teach Advisors that Activity Solves All Problems** — Al Granum's One Card System is timeless and applies to experienced as well as new advisors.

- **Use Professional Designations as Proof of Commitment** — Advisors and leaders in our profession should offer their clients nothing less than professionalism and a commitment to lifelong learning.

- **"What You Cannot Avoid, Welcome"** — As this Chinese proverb suggests, change is inevitable, and growth is our choice. Coach your advisors to get out of their comfort zones and into growth opportunities.

Chapter 23

Expect Only What You Inspect

A RULE OF THUMB that I have followed throughout my career is, "If you can measure it, you can manage it. If you can't measure it, you can't manage it." I learned this key principle from a LAMP presentation made by John Lefferts of AXA Equitable.

As leaders, our targets should always be quantifiable so that we can measure them against our original plan. Having concrete data to track and inspect allows us to monitor our progress. We should expect results only in those areas where we have set quantifiable, measurable goals.

Metrics Help You Inspect

Metrics are the standards by which you measure your own performance or the performance of your advisors and the other team members within your organization.

The last chapter, Quarterly Reviews, contains examples of metrics that we use to measure *advisor* performance. You also need to establish metrics to measure *organizational* performance.

Recently, I read that every organization needs four to six metrics, or standards, by which it measures its performance. Once you get 9, 10 or 11 metrics, you simply have too many. You lose focus when you're distracted by spinning so many plates. You have to simplify your metrics as much as possible.

North Star has four key metrics:

1. **Recruiting** — We set an annual goal and measure against it monthly. In 2006, our goal was to hire 27 new advisors.

2. **Retention** — Our goal is to have a 50 percent four-year retention rate, and we review quarterly reports that show where we are in relation to this goal.

3. **Persistency** — We measure how much of our business stays on the books beyond 39 months, and that number cannot be and never has been below 93 percent. Our responsibility is to keep that 93 percent metric in place. (Every 1 percent increase in a company's persistency translates to a 5 percent increase in its bottom-line profitability to stockholders or to policyholder dividends.)

4. **Life Insurance Sales** — This is our most important metric. We came into this business to change lives, and life insurance is the single product that enables us to do that the best and the most frequently. Our metric is a minimum of $550,000 of commission per month. We know our average volume per dollar of commission, and that tells us how much life insurance in force we have. Then we break that down on a per-advisor basis, which then becomes a metric of supervision.

Execution

Three frogs are sitting on a lily pad. One decides to jump off. How many are left? Three. You see, deciding to jump off doesn't change anything. You've got to actually *do* it. That's where execution comes in. After you come up with your plan, you have to follow through with it.

As leaders, we can be successful only if we execute our plan and monitor our results against our goals. In the final analysis, execution of our plan will determine whether we win or lose.

Once you have decided on your plan and have committed it to writing — and it's always important to commit it to writing — then you need to do periodic monitoring to determine what progress has been made and how that progress compares to your plan.

For example, if your recruiting goal was 24 hires for the year, and you're going to spread those evenly throughout the year, then on January 31, you need to make sure that you've hired two advisors for the month. Who was responsible for it? What did they say they were going to do? Did they do it? If not, why not? And what activity are they going to change in the future to bring about a different result from the one that was not sufficient in January?

If you can measure it, you can manage it. Many recruiters are unable to quantify the most basic aspects of their recruiting efforts. Can you?

Recruiting Numbers for (Year)

No. of first interviews conducted	_____
No. of career presentations made	_____
No. of tests given	_____
No. of tests returned	_____
No. of candidates recommended for hire	_____
No. of offers made	_____
No. of acceptances	_____

Accountability

People love accountability. They love goals, they love holding themselves accountable and they love having others hold them accountable as well. When you inspect what's being done in your organization, you're creating opportunities to catch people doing something right and to shower them with compliments, which are really verbal sunshine.

On the third day of January each year, our advisors love getting a note from their field leader saying, "What a year you had! Congratulations. You really worked hard, and it came together for you. We hope the success that you feel matches the pride that we feel in what you have accomplished."

And we field leaders love getting that same type of note from our company CEOs. We're being held accountable to certain standards; we've met those standards and now we're being rewarded in more than a monetary way for meeting or exceeding them.

As field leaders, we all have grand expectations of what success looks like in our firms. We can turn these expectations into reality by inspecting what we expect. And by monitoring the key metrics of our firm's performance, we will be able to tell if we're winning or losing.

> *Quality is never an accident; it is always the result of high intention, sincere effort, intelligent direction and skillful execution; it represents the wise choice of many alternatives.*
>
> WILLIAM A. FOSTER

You Take the Helm

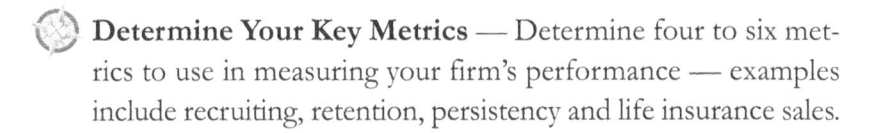

- **Determine Your Key Metrics** — Determine four to six metrics to use in measuring your firm's performance — examples include recruiting, retention, persistency and life insurance sales.

- **Develop Your Plan, Then Execute It** — Formulating your plan, writing it down and communicating it are only the beginning. It's the *execution* of your plan that will lead to the desired results.

- **Measure It to Manage It** — Monitor the key metrics of your firm's operation and adjust as needed to succeed.

- **Expect Only What You Inspect** — Likewise, inspect only what you expect.

Chapter 24

Live Where You Want, With Those You Love, Doing the Right Work, On Purpose

THROUGHOUT this book, we talk about the importance of creating a business that you are proud to be a part of and putting all of the pieces in place to make that happen. It is just as important to your personal happiness and success for you to create the life that you were meant to live and to put all of the pieces in place to make it happen.

The four very important points in the title of this chapter are from *Repacking Your Bags*.[1] In that great book, authors Richard Leider and David Shapiro say that the formula for the good life is "living in the place you belong, with the people you love, doing the right work, on purpose." They explain the importance of integrating these vital components of our lives, much like the blended approach we discussed in Chapter 12.

---

[1] Richard J. Leider and David A. Shapiro, *Repacking Your Bags: Lighten Your Load for the Rest of Your Life,* Berrett-Koehler Publishers, San Francisco, 1995, p. 26.

Quality of life is not a matter of chance. It is the result of searching for and identifying the reason we are here. We are hard-wired to want to know the purpose for our life. Without purpose, we become a dangling participle looking for a subject to modify.

I remember sitting in dorm rooms in college, hearing fellow students say, "What really is happiness?" and "When I have it, how will I really know it?" And I often hear advisors say, "I don't know if I'm really happy now. I don't know that I'm not happy, but how would I know, if I have nothing to compare it to?" When I read those points by Leider and Shapiro, it was an epiphany. There for the first time was the answer to that age-old question about what happiness is, and in a form that I could memorize, repeat and fall in love with.

If you're doing these four things, I believe that you've arrived: living wherever you want to live, with the people you really love, doing the right work, and purposefully — not accidentally, not because you happened to fall into it, but because it really is what you want to do.

No one has a better opportunity to grasp these components of the good life than the advisors in our industry and the field leaders who guide those advisors. As I look at the professions of people with whom I'm very close — physicians, clergy, lawyers, salespeople, senior vice presidents, board members, chairmen of the boards of publicly traded companies — I see that none of them have a better opportunity than we do to live wherever we want to live, with the people we love, doing the right work, on purpose.

With today's technology, our advisors can do just what my advisor Eric Seybert is doing. He has physician clients around the country and works out of his house in Bozeman, Montana. He lives where he wants to live with the people he loves — his wife and two children — doing the right work, which is helping his clients, and he is doing it purposefully. He's a happy guy. You don't get any happier than that. He is responsible to himself.

As the field leaders who coach and guide advisors, we have that same flexibility. Do you know any physicians who can do that? Any lawyers? I don't. I don't know anybody who can do that as well as the people who distribute our miraculous product.

This incomparable opportunity to work in our industry is available to just about anybody, not just a select few. Many of us reap the benefits of working in this industry. We drink from wells dug by those who went before us. We live where we want, with those we love, doing the right work, on purpose. We are changing lives, forever.

> *It is the paradox of life that the way to miss pleasure is to seek it first. The very first condition of lasting happiness is that a life should be full of purpose, aiming at something outside self.*
>
> HUGH BLACK

Chapter 25

Think Tombstones

What Is Your Leadership Legacy?

IN CHAPTER 1, we talked about how having a strong vision helps you decide where you're headed — it allows you to begin with the end in mind.

One night, I was lying in bed thinking about the concept of beginning with the end in mind. I wondered, if I were to write my own eulogy, what would I say about my life? And what epitaph on my tombstone would summarize the impact of my life? What difference did I make while I was here? Why is the world better off because I passed through?

I decided that on my tombstone I want an epitaph composed of three simple words; not even my name, just "He grew people."

This tombstone exercise forces us to think about our life's purpose and the legacy we want to leave — personally, professionally and as parents. It compels us to make decisions about the kind of life and business we need to construct so we will achieve that legacy.

Imagine Your Legacy

Author Stephen Covey says that the most fundamental application of beginning with the end in mind is to begin today with the image, picture or paradigm of the end of your life as your frame of reference or the criterion by which everything else is examined. He suggests that you examine each part of your life — your behavior today, tomorrow, next week, next month and so on — in the context of what really matters most to you. By keeping that end clearly in mind, you can make certain that everything you do contributes in a meaningful way to the vision you have of your life as a whole.[1]

Swedish chemist Alfred Nobel made a fortune by inventing dynamite. In April 1888, a French newspaper reported that Nobel had died at age 57 after a heart attack. The article described him as a "merchant of death," a man whose enormous wealth came mainly from devising innovative ways to "mutilate and kill" thousands. But it was not Alfred Nobel who had died, it was his brother Ludvig. The newspaper had made a mistake.[2]

When Alfred Nobel read the obituary, he realized that he needed to make changes. He did not want to be remembered as a merchant of death. He decided to devote his life and fortune to humanity and to the recognition of those who excel in humanitarian efforts. He rewrote his will to establish the Nobel prizes for people who further the humanities through their contributions to science and the arts. His life changed from one extreme to another because he imagined his own obituary.

Live Your Mission

Our mission statement at North Star Resource Group is "Changing Lives, Forever®." My advisors would be honored if you were to suggest that they change lives *for the better*, that they change lives

---

[1]Stephen R. Covey, *The 7 Habits of Highly Effective People: Powerful Lessons in Personal Change*, Simon & Schuster, New York, 1989, p. 98.
[2]John Bankston, *Alfred Nobel and the Story of the Nobel Prize (The Great Achiever Awards)*, Mitchell Lane Publishers, Inc.: Hockessin, Delaware, 2004, p. 1.

forever. They want nothing more than to know that people whose loved ones died were able to stay in their neighborhoods and continue going to the same schools and places of worship because they had helped that family plan ahead. They would probably like the idea of "He changed lives" or "She changed lives" as an epitaph. And our advisors do change lives. Because of their efforts, North Star paid out more than $20 million in death claims each year during this century.

Premature death without preparation is more than unfortunate; it is a tragedy for those left behind who must fend for themselves. Most people in this business want to help others avoid that tragedy. We want to know that men will someday be called "elderly gentlemen" because we helped them send money into the future to take care of themselves, that people don't have to become part-time parents when their spouses die and that people who become disabled retain their dignity and the respect of others in their community because they were prudent enough to manage their risks properly. The life insurance advisor is the fortune teller who tells you exactly what is going to happen, and it always does.

People don't instinctively or voluntarily do these things for themselves. But when a life insurance advisor shows them a better way, it resonates with people of character. They implement that suggestion. And when they do, you can say that the advisor has "changed lives forever."

Titles or Testimonies?

At LAMP 1989, Dr. Anthony Campolo delivered a general session presentation called "Titles or Testimonies." Dr. Campolo is a Baptist minister and a professor emeritus at Eastern College in St. Davids, Pennsylvania. He spoke of asking some young students at his church what they wanted to become in life. He listened to each child's answer. Then he said, "Now, you children listen up. One day you're going to die. You don't think you're going to die, but you are going to die, and they're going to drop you into a hole and go back to the church and eat potato salad. And they're going to stand around and talk about you. What they say about you will depend on what you lived for. Did you live for titles or testimonies?"

That is a pretty hefty concept for children, but it's one that adults need to consider. Do we want to spend our time and energy acquiring status, or do we want to live a life of meaning and testimony?

I think those who are involved in the sale of life insurance have demonstrated that they've chosen to live a life of testimony. There are few testimonies greater than the work we do every day to intercede in the lives of our fellow human beings to offer help at the precise moment when they need it.

What is the legacy you want to leave?

> *Do not fear death so much, but rather the inadequate life.*
> BERTOLT BRECHT

Epilogue

Our Industry Today

WHILE SOME aspects of the insurance and financial services industry remain just as they were when I started my career in 1962, dramatic changes have also taken place. Many of these changes have improved the industry, but unfortunately some of them have been detrimental to face-to-face distribution.

We can overcome the impacts posed by these damaging trends if we pull together as an industry. The first step is to recognize the serious challenges that we face.

Our Two Biggest Challenges

At the 2003 Joint Executives Committee meeting, industry executives identified the two most significant threats that are negatively affecting the insurance-based sector of the financial services industry:

- The shrinking number of agents and advisors entering the industry
- The growing but increasingly underserved middle-income market in this country

To address these challenges, the committee launched an initiative called the Task Force for the Future, one of the most significant collaborations in the history of the insurance-based financial services industry. The Task Force was charged with quantifying these threats and identifying remedies. Charlie Smith, who was GAMA International's CEO from 1998-2003 and is one of my fellow inductees into the Management Hall of Fame, provided stellar direction and insight as the founding chairman of this Task Force.

After two meetings in 2004, the Task Force developed a comprehensive report, which revealed the following difficult truths about the state of our industry.[1]

- The industry has shifted its product focus away from life insurance.
- Individual term life insurance is quickly becoming the leading life insurance product, while the value, uniqueness and relevance of permanent life insurance is being marginalized.
- Over the last 30 years, the industry has lost 80,000 affiliated agents, severely threatening our capacity and commitment to build face-to-face distribution.
- Because of a smaller field force and an expanding population, fewer middle-income households own life insurance than ever before. This makes it more difficult for us to defend the tax advantages of permanent life insurance, erodes our industry's grassroots political support and marginalizes its social mandate to serve the protection needs of all Americans.

In one of the last articles that he wrote as CEO of LIMRA International, Rich Wecker called this situation "the perfect storm":

> I've never witnessed a shipwreck, but we've all seen the movie *Titanic*, so I think I have some idea how it goes. The fatal wound in the dark, the confusion and panic, the final descent beneath the waves, all played out in relentless slow motion to the inevitable conclusion. Am I talking about the life insurance industry? I certainly hope — and truly believe — that will not be our fate. But I think we must acknowledge that we have a gash below the waterline that needs to be fixed so we don't, in fact, end up like the *Titanic*. That gash, this potentially fatal weakness, is the middle market — millions of average citizens earning a decent living who want

---

[1] Charles S. Smith, CLU ChFC, "The Task Force for the Future: Navigating the Perfect Storm," *GAMA International Journal*, March/April 2005; also available on www.gamaweb.com.

and need life insurance, but for a variety of reasons, are not getting it.[2]

The Task Force acknowledged that all segments of the industry are responsible for the peril we face. On a personal note, I think we owe a debt of gratitude to the multiline companies in America today because any success we do have in the mid-market is largely due to their efforts.

The Task Force also agreed that it is the collective responsibility of all segments of the industry to contribute to solutions. Members identified four primary elements of the transformation that need to take place:

- An industry-wide commitment to provide adequate life insurance protection to all Americans, acknowledging that the most effective means to accomplish this is through face-to-face distribution

- A significant investment by the companies in recruiting and training advisors for face-to-face distribution

- An effective execution by field management in recruiting and training advisors for face-to-face distribution

- A significant engagement by every field organization to solve this problem[3]

I am now serving as co-chair of the Task Force for the Future, along with Richard Koob, a financial representative with Northwestern Mutual, and Henry Hagan, president and CEO of Monumental Life Insurance Company. I'm involved because I believe that it is our collective responsibility as field leaders to arrest this decline and steer the ship away from the iceberg. I'm positive that we can. There are many aspects of our industry that we can control. We need more companies and field leaders to recommit to a focus on life insurance

---

[2]Smith, *GAMA International Journal*.
[3]Smith, *GAMA International Journal*.

as the flywheel that drives client relationships. We need more field leaders to share their best practices and ideas with others in our industry so that we can build stronger organizations. We need to continue to invest in recruiting and training new advisors in order to stop the proselytizing that is cannibalizing our industry. And we need to continue to professionalize our industry and provide a structured and nurturing environment that will help us retain those advisors and compete with the independent broker dealers.

One person who has done a lion's share of the work in turning our industry around is David Woods. David has worked in the insurance industry for more than 40 years. He was a life insurance agent for 30 of those years and has been a member of the Million Dollar Round Table since 1970. Currently, he is the Chief Executive Officer of the National Association of Insurance and Financial Advisors (NAIFA) and also served as NAIFA's president from 1986-87. David assumed leadership of NAIFA during turbulent times, in the midst of the greatest changes ever to take place in that organization's 117-year history. Also the current president of the Life and Health Insurance Foundation for Education (LIFE), David continues the quest to educate the public about the value and necessity of life insurance. In addition, David served on the original Task Force for the Future, and he has served on the Boards of Directors of both the Association for Advanced Life Underwriting and The American College. David is just one of many servant leaders who play a key role in strengthening our industry. The collective efforts of all involved have now resulted in agreement by the ACLI with the goals and mission of the task force. I applaud all of you and thank you. I know that together, we can turn this ship around. This book is my contribution to that vital mission.

Barbarians at the Gate

One of the statistics that the Task Force for the Future discovered was that between 1998 and 2001, the number of life brokers/personal producing general agents (PPGAs) increased by 48,000. In 2003, 52 percent of premium was sold through the independent channel, 38 percent was sold by affiliated agents and 10 percent was categorized as "other."

We have had personal experience with the loss of career advisors to independent broker dealers. At the end of our most recent fiscal year, which ended June 30, North Star lost 16 percent of our total production from the previous year because advisors left to go with independent broker dealers. This has never happened to us before.

If you've seen the Roman Coliseum, you've noticed that the walls are higher in some parts than they are in others. They are that way because for many centuries following the fall of Rome, Romans and other Italians used the coliseum as a marble quarry. They would take huge chunks of marble from the Coliseum and use them to build their homes, palaces, castles, roads and other things.

That is a perfect analogy for what independent broker dealers are doing to our industry right now — proselytizing our advisors. Our industry must recognize, soon, that these barbarians at our gate are stealing our people, causing our turnover to go up and our persistency as firms and agencies, as companies, and as an industry, to go down. More important, though, this trend is not in the best interests of our policyholders.

At industry meetings, I often hear people say that other insurance companies are our competition. I have always taken the position that insurance companies are not one another's competitors. Our true competitors are the independent broker dealers. They are coming after successful agents in our firms and agencies (some have as many as 20 full-time recruiters canvassing the marketplace) offering them anywhere from 90 to 98 percent of the broker dealer concession — in effect, 98 percent of all the comp there is to be paid.

That *sounds* like a lot, when you consider that we are paying out 55 to 60 percent, including all bonuses. But the broker dealers are telling only half of the story. They are not giving our advisors the full details about the many expenses that will cut significantly into that nominal profit.

Will Leitch cited a Cerulli Associates study in the article "Indie Existentialism — Is the Independent Life Really Worth Living?"

appearing in the June 2004 issue of *Registered Rep* magazine. The study found that independent broker dealers spend as much as 40 percent of their working time managing the business. This cuts drastically into the amount of time that advisors can spend with clients. The article went on to say that, "Further, the payout figures do not account for the costs of starting an independent office, which most reps will tell you is the biggest financial drain of all."

In the *E Myth Revisited*, Gerber talks about how technicians are involved with the here and now, entrepreneurs are involved with the vision and tomorrow and managers are involved with a little bit of today, but a lot of the past, in terms of making their businesses work. When advisors sign on with an independent broker dealer, they're going to have to perform all three of those roles.[4]

So the 90 to 98 percent concessions that the broker dealers are boasting about are gross, not net, concessions. An advisor's actual profit will typically end up being around 55 percent, which is equal to or less than the 55 to 60 percent that we were paying them when they decided to leave.

Gerber also talks about how greed will be one's downfall. He says, "If all you want from a business of your own is the opportunity to do what you did before, get paid more for it, and have more freedom to come and go, your greed – I know that sounds harsh, but that's what it is – your self-indulgence will eventually consume both you and your business."[5]

So advisors may get more money at the top end, but all of a sudden they're not going to be working *on* their business anymore. They're going to be working *in* their business in more ways than they ever dreamed necessary — paying rent, meeting payroll, hiring and firing people, filling out forms, doing tax returns and workers' comp forms, dealing with hospital and major medical insurance, working with compliance officers. These tasks are not fully discussed during

---

[4] Michael Gerber, *The E Myth Revisited: Why Most Small Businesses Don't Work and What to Do About It*, HarperCollins: New York, 1995, pp. 19–33.
[5] Ibid, p. 41.

recruiting interviews when broker dealers proselytize affiliated agents.

In contrast, a successful advisor in a career agency system really only has to involve himself or herself in being a good technician — loving people, loving to be with them, loving to help them and loving financial planning.

While our industry has not fully responded to the challenge presented by the independent broker dealers, we do have significant advantages, specifically product manufacturing and what I refer to as *staff privileges*.

Product Manufacturing

The strategic advantage of the insurance industry is in the manufacture of the product. That's where insurance companies make their money, not in the distribution. The subsidiary broker dealer that is owned by the insurance company does not have to be a profit center as does the independent broker dealer. As more of the independents become public corporations, the need for more return on equity will increase.

At a 2006 meeting of the industry's Executive Management Cabinet, John Greene, president of agency distribution for the Prudential Life Insurance Company of America, said, "We think of our broker dealer as a utility now, striving for break-even, but not imprisoned by that demand." Independent broker dealers do not manufacture any products, so they don't have any manufacturing profits. What I have been preaching for some time, and what John Greene has now said, is that manufacturers — the insurance companies that own their broker dealers — don't have to make a profit on the broker dealer distribution system.

Independent broker dealers are at a strategic disadvantage. Their acquisition costs are high, and they face ongoing external pressure to show significant profits on those acquisitions. They are publicly traded companies, with Wall Street coming in every 90 days to see what their profits are and demanding as much as a 15 percent or more return on investment.

Insurance companies are just now beginning to understand that the broker dealer housing their agents is a utility of the insurance company. It is the way they distribute products, but it is not a profit center. If you look at the entire package — the manufacturing profits along with the broker dealer distribution costs — the business is profitable.

This was the conclusion we came to at North Star but we wanted to make sure that we did not miss something and fall victim to wishful thinking. That's why in 2006, North Star engaged the well-known consulting firm Moss Adams to perform a detailed comparison of the North Star compensation paid to advisors and the compensation available from independent broker dealers. Moss Adams performs a number of surveys amongst advisors and they came to the engagement with a large database of financial statements from independent advisors. Now our advisors could finally see what actually occurs in real independent broker dealer firms, not just a theoretical income model.

The findings largely validated what we believed from the start — the compensation of advisors inside our agency model was not only competitive with the independent broker dealers but in many cases was the highest available of all models. The research included nine of the leading independent broker dealers and considered four different profiles of advisors. The profiles incorporated different levels of total production by the advisor and different mixes of business — we did not want to be myopic and focus only on life insurance. We really wanted to make sure that our model is rewarding to a broad range of advisors.

In their analysis, the consultants from Moss Adams looked at every single expense item in an independent practice and the expenses that our housed advisors incur in order to scrutinize every detail of both the top-line and the bottom-line compensation.

What they found was that North Star compensation was 4 percent higher than the highest independent broker dealer compensation for our Chairman's Club advisors (production over $600,000), 6 percent higher than the highest independent broker dealer compensation for our life insurance-focused advisors (those who have two thirds of their business in life premium) and that for other advisors, North Star was within 7 percent of the highest compensation offered by a broker dealer — a result that the consultants described as "competitive."

Why is our compensation so attractive when our payout is lower? The answer is simple — in the analysis performed, the independent broker dealer practices spent over 43 percent of their revenue on overhead — rent, staff, infrastructure, external help, etc. — services that the housed advisor finds inside the firm. More important, housed advisors realize significant economies of scale and leverage from the size of the agency.

When Moss Adams presented their results to our advisors, one advisor in the audience asked a very smart question, "How come we only have one-half of a dedicated assistant when the independent guys have a full time person supporting them?" The answer? "Consider all of the people in the agency supporting you — the receptionist, the IT people, the compliance people, marketing support, the accounting department, etc. You are not supported by just one-half of an assistant, you are supported by many people — many more than one full-time equivalent. The real question is, 'How does the independent guy get it done with just one person who has to be a receptionist, IT expert, compliance person and so on?'"

That's the economic advantage of the agency model — the efficiency and leverage of the shared resources and the quality of these resources. North Star has a Value Proposition that we share with advisors that illustrates the resources and benefits we provide. (See the Appendix.)

There are other components that I wish the consultants could quantify — How much time does an independent advisor waste on compliance, administration and other tasks that we provide to advisors? What is the quality of the support they get from the one person they can afford to hire as opposed to the many professionals we have? Isn't it a little lonely being all by yourself with no one to talk to, no one to learn from and no one to ask for advice? These are valuable, though intangible, components of our model. But as we saw in the research, the model stands on its own even without these answers. (Additional information about the Moss Adams findings is included in the Appendix.)

Staff Privileges

The independent broker dealers have told our advisors, "You are compromised because you are affiliated with a company that manufactures a product." They are implying that our advisors can only sell that company's products. And in some isolated cases, that may be true. But most companies do not follow that model. Most companies allow their advisors to place business with another quality company to achieve their clients' best interests. This argument discounts the professionalism of advisors to do the right thing, as well as their commitment to the CLU oath.

Our advisors are not compelled to put all of their business with Minnesota Mutual. What they are compelled to do is to put the interests of their clients first.

To use a medical metaphor again, my advisors are similar to doctors who have an affiliation, or staff privileges, with a hospital. They are going to refer their patients back to their own hospital, except in extreme cases when another hospital excels in the particular discipline in which the patient's need lies. In such a case, you can bet that the physician will refer the patient to the well-known specialty hospital. But when you go to an "independent" physician who has no staff privileges at the hospital you need to go to, he cannot treat you there. You now need to find another physician to be your primary advocate because your physician cannot practice in that hospital without staff privileges.

That scenario runs parallel to my advisors being able to call up our own underwriters and say, "This client also has this business with us, and I need you to work the re-insurance companies harder to get me a better rating than the one you've offered me." You can do that when you're in your own "staff hospital."

Because we have staff privileges, we can also get a policy loan check written for a client on short notice. Many times, we have clients who will call our advisors and say something like, "I need $30,000 immediately." We can call Securian's policy service department and have a check shipped overnight to our client so that he or she receives it the next day.

Independent broker dealers are less able to provide these exceptional services because they don't have staff privileges.

My Predictions for the Industry's Future

I would like to share a dozen predictions for our future based on my industry involvement over four decades and on my position as co-chair of the industry's Task Force for the Future.

You'll see that my predictions assume the continued influence that our trusted advisors — not independent broker dealers — have on their clients' financial-planning and life-planning decisions. Many of these trends are already under way and will accelerate. Others will be the result of the dynamics caused by those trends. As you read, bear in mind the Chinese proverb, "What you cannot avoid, welcome."

1. Commission compression will continue as manufacturers (life insurers) search for ways to shave production costs. Case in point: In 1965, $100,000 of permanent life insurance for a 45-year-old male to age 100 cost $3,799 per year; today, it costs only $1,362.

2. Consolidation of companies, firms and advisor practices will occur more frequently to achieve necessary economies of scale.

3. Pressure for transparency and commission disclosure will continue to increase, thus reducing some of the challenges of commission compression.

4. Commission disclosure will benefit the consumer in the near term and will help consumers, companies, and advisors in the long term.

5. Solo practitioners as well as small offices will be fewer and more challenged by their small scale in an environment of increasing costs and by compliance considerations. (Small offices are the 16,407 firms managing under $25 million in assets, according to filings with the SEC, and even the 2,607 who manage under $100 million in assets.)

6. Advisors will gradually make fees for service an increasing part of their practices, though for most, not exclusively.

7. Commoditization of products will exert additional pressure on prices, causing further pressure on commissions.

8. Specialization will accelerate among advisors who form strategic alliances, allowing each to focus on their unique skills, gifts and passions. At the same time, the breadth of product offerings will increase through cross-marketing.

9. Advisors will continue to earn more as they develop more efficient strategies to maximize their scale, such as specialization, delegation and profile marketing.

10. Life planning will expand, with advisors increasingly in a consultative role as the trusted advisor. This will include, but will not be limited to, financial planning.

11. Financial planning will continue to be among the most desirable vocations in the nation. The shift to more balance between men and women in our industry will accelerate and the increase in the number of people of color in our industry will better reflect the demographic trends now in place.

12. The trusted advisor will continue to evolve into the lynchpin for a stronger America by creating long-term savings, secure retirement via long-term care and annuities and financial independence for clients through risk-avoidance products such as life insurance and disability income. The life insurance industry already provides one-third of the long-term savings in the United States.

The Miracle of Life Insurance

I began my career in this industry learning about the miracle of life insurance from Maury Stewart, so it's only befitting that I end this book about my industry experience on a positive note. What could be more positive than a product that materializes at precisely the moment it is needed in the family of a person who has died?

When a trusted advisor brings up the difficult subject of mortality to clients and suggests the purchase of a life insurance policy, and when those clients have the wisdom and character to heed the advisor's suggestion, their family's future is made more secure. Life insurance provides an individual with peace of mind, and it provides their loved ones with the means to continue their current lifestyle upon that person's death.

Here is an example of the miracle of life insurance in action.

In January 2004, two of North Star's associates, Tony Andreason and Scott Gislason, succeeded in convincing three business partners to each purchase $1 million in buy-and-sell life insurance. One of the business owners, a 44-year-old who had never used alcohol or drugs, eaten meat, or had any reason to ever visit a physician, believed himself to be immortal. Scott and Tony overcame his objections, and drew up the policies for all three men.

(Because of the incredible nature of the one man's background, you might imagine how difficult it was for Minnesota Life to underwrite him, but this was finally achieved.)

Only eight months later, in October 2004, the 10-month-old life policy matured with an explosion of money precisely when it was needed: a car accident ended the man's life. While it was the worst of times, Tony and Scott delivered $1 million to his partners. Their jobs, as well as those of other employees, were saved.

In talking with Scott and Tony about the case later, I was fascinated by their description of the tipping point that finally made the businessman buy the policy. Somewhere in the midst of the deliberations, a light went on in his head. He realized that the proceeds go to the ones who live, so it is really insurance for the living — that's why they call it life insurance. He got it. And because he got it, the lives of others were changed forever.

That's what we do at North Star, and that's what all of us in this industry do. We change lives, forever.

Appendix

Chapter 4 Sample Documents	**Page**
North Star Offer Letter	234
North Star Letter to Parents	235
North Star Letter of Intent	236
North Star Letter of Commitment	237
North Star Mentoring Agreement	241
North Star Apprentice/Mentor Split Case Agreement	242
North Star New Associate Apprenticeship Program	244

Chapter 22 Sample Documents	**Page**
North Star Quarterly Review Questionnaire	246

Epilogue Sample Documents	**Page**
North Star Value Proposition	248
North Star Moss Adams Findings Article	251
North Star Moss Adams Report Excerpt	253

North Star Offer Letter

Dear ,

It is with great pleasure that I would like to formally welcome you to the North Star Resource Group family. You should feel extremely proud of your accomplishment of getting through our extremely selective interviewing process. North Star Resource Group is recognized in the financial services industry as being one of the most selective firms in the country. By receiving an offer to join our firm, you have displayed the entrepreneurial spirit, leadership skills and discipline needed to excel in this career.

The next few months will be extremely challenging, at times frustrating, but most of all rewarding. Building your own financial planning practice is something few people have the opportunity to do with the caliber of a firm such as North Star Resource Group. You are about to embark on a career path which can help you obtain the three "I's" which most people seek in a rewarding, fulfilling career. Those three "I's" are, having Impact on your client's lives, creating Independence for yourself, and lastly giving yourself the opportunity to have Income very few achieve in life. But in order to accomplish this you must be willing to work the long hours, face the rejection and stay focused on the tasks at hand that North Star presents you. Kelsey Dumke, Contracts and Licensing Administrator and Tracie LaRue, Training Coordinator, will contact you to complete the necessary paperwork.

Once again I would like to congratulate you. I am extremely proud of your accomplishments thus far. I look forward to seeing you receive many awards throughout your illustrious career, but most of all I look forward to seeing you reach your own goals and objectives and helping your clients reach theirs.

Kindest regards,

Edward G. Deutschlander, CLU, CLF
Executive Vice President

North Star Letter to Parents

Dear ,

Congratulations! North Star Resource Group has offered your daughter the opportunity to join one of the largest and oldest independent financial services firms in the industry. At North Star our mission is simple: Changing Lives, Forever®. As a training firm we recognize that our aim is to grow the best and brightest financial advisors. At North Star, Ann will begin a career development program that we have created to transition new advisors into the industry. Through working with a mentor, participating in our education programs, and building a client base, Ann will have the opportunity to change her life and the lives of her clients, forever. We recognize that you are a major part of her life and are therefore part of the extended North Star family. We would like to educate you as well about the career opportunity, our history and our values. We have included some information about North Star for you to explore. Our door is always open and we would be happy to answer any questions or address any concerns that you may have. Please feel free to contact us in the future.

Best Wishes,

Ed Deutschlander, CLU, CLF
Executive Vice President

North Star Letter of Intent

Dear :

Congratulations on your recent offer as an Associate with North Star Resource Group. We are very proud of our track record of having very successful advisors at our firm.

As our Chairman, Phil Richards has stated, "You will be overworked and underpaid for the first five years of your career and then most likely will be overpaid and underworked for the rest of your career."

The only thing that can stop you from succeeding in this career is you deciding not to get back up when this business knocks you down. This will most likely be the most difficult challenge you have ever faced.

We have found that people tend to live up to what they write down. We are asking for your firm commitment that you are willing to do everything it takes and commit yourself to five years as an advisor with North Star Resource Group. For this reason we would like to have your word that you are firmly committed to giving five years of hard work to this career. North Star's investment in you through the first 5 years will exceed $250,000. The greatest portion of this investment is in the first 2 years.

I _____, agree to commit to five years of difficulty to establish a career with North Star Resource Group.

_____

Signed   Date

North Star Letter of Commitment

In anticipation of building a successful career and to achieve the goals that we strive for together, North Star Resource Group makes the following commitments to you:

- To provide a high-performance/no-excuse culture that will assist you in building a world-class financial advising practice.
- To provide an Apprenticeship program whereby a mentor is assigned to each apprentice.
- To provide a success-oriented, positive environment for those in the North Star Apprenticeship program.
- To provide quality office conditions that are conducive to building a successful practice.
- To provide quality training and development through firm, company and industry methods.
- To provide the highest level of individualized supervision on a weekly, monthly and quarterly basis.
- To provide the highest standards of education, product, technology, management and administrative support.
- To provide the resources that will enable you to develop the practice you desire and have a prosperous career as a member of the North Star family.
- To provide the greatest support network in the industry allowing our advisors to be "relationship managers" and giving them the confidence that our specialists can assist their clients regardless of the complexity of the client's situation.

In exchange, we ask you for a number of commitments that are imperative for your success at North Star Resource Group:

- **Must pass all insurance and securities exams prior to your official start date.** As a representative of North Star Resource Group, an associate must be fully licensed and contracted prior to starting any formal training class (see attached).
- Until licensed, must participate in North Star's Marketing Representative Program.**
- Advancement to Quick Start Program.***
  – Pass Insurance and Securities Exams.

- Hold 10-20 Center of Influence (COI)/Natural Market recommendation gathering meetings with Mentor.
- Obtain 100 Qualified recommendations.

- Advancement to Career Development Program (CDP).
  - Submission of 10 applications (Life insurance, disability insurance or annuity).
- Become LEAP licensed and practice LEAP as your Financial Advising process.
- To conduct yourself at all times understanding that you are an "ambassador" for North Star Resource Group and uphold our long and well deserved reputation as an industry leader.
- To attend all functions that your manager recommends.
- To maintain the following objectives:
  - To secure appointments.
  - To conduct appointments.
  - To master the art of asking for recommendations/introductions.
  - To master telling the North Star Story.
  - Appreciate and acknowledge Life Insurance as the cornerstone of any financial design.
  - To master the importance of Human Life Value.
  - To work with your mentor/manager as he or she recommends in any capacity.
  - To achieve the goal of gold validation under the CDP contract.
  - To become a member of NAIFA.

- To meet with your mentor/manager on a weekly basis and supply weekly activity reports.
- To meet with your Regional Vice President on a quarterly basis.
- To meet with one of the Managing Partners on a quarterly basis.
- To follow the policy and procedures of North Star Resource Group and to strive toward the highest levels of production, integrity and confidentiality.
- It is through following these practices and the other goals and objectives set by you and North Star Resource Group that you will gold validate each and every period of your CDP contract and be on target to be a member of the Million Dollar Round Table at the end of your third year as a North Star Advisor.

We are proud to have you as a member of our family. A great deal of time has been put into our selection of one another. We are signing this letter to indicate our commitment to you and we ask that you sign it as your commitment to us.

Edward G. Deutschlander   Date

Associate   Date

All offers made to North Star Resource Group advisors are contingent on the candidate meeting the necessary contracting and licensing requirements and completion of four-month **North Star Marketing Representative Program PRIOR TO THE CAREER DEVELOPMENT PROGRAM START DATE. Any failure to meet this requirement allows for immediate termination and voids any employment contract with North Star Resource Group.

Current requirements are that the candidate complete the necessary instructional component as well as pass the required insurance and security exams needed to represent North Star Resource Group in that particular state in which they will be housed. It is also required that the candidate be contracted with The Minnesota Life Insurance Company, CRI Securities, and Marathon Advisors.

One should allow a minimum of eight to twelve weeks to complete all the licensing and contracting components assuming they pass all exams on the first attempt. NASD requires a thirty-day waiting period before sitting for the Series 6 or 7 exam if one is unsuccessful after the first attempt. If a candidate is unsuccessful passing the Series 6 or 7 after three attempts in any given year they have a six-month waiting period.

Our recommendation to all candidates that have received contingent offers is that they take the licensing and contracting very seriously and work with a North Star Resource Group management member in designing a timeline to assist them in meeting the licensing and contracting requirements. North Star Resource

Group is not responsible for anyone missing the training class start date due to testing, licensing, or contracting issues.

**North Star Marketing Representative Program:
While obtaining Life and Securities Licenses, you are responsible for securing Center of Influence (COI)/Natural Market meetings to be held with your mentor to obtain 100 qualified referrals. You will position your licensed trainer/mentor for these meetings as you will be operating in the Relationship Manager capacity and legally cannot make recommendations.

***You are responsible for all costs associated with contracting and licensing. After successfully completing your first validation period (CDP months 1-4) you will receive a $2,000.00 bonus to be used as reimbursement for the costs associated with contracts and licensing.

North Star Mentoring Agreement

This Mentor Program has been established as a means of supporting the growth and development of new advisors by pairing them with experienced Associates. This business agreement places certain obligations and responsibilities on both parties:

- New Associate must communicate with his or her Mentor daily. The primary purpose being the learning environment for individual case study, client preparation and product recommendation.
- New Associate must email his or her daily activity at the end of the day for the first three periods to RVP, Mentor, Ed Deutschlander and Tracie LaRue.
- All appointments held with Mentor during first three periods of the Career Development Program. Any requests to work with Associates, other than Mentor must be approved by Mentor and Management Team.
- Commissions:
  – Joint client's split 50/50 for the life of the client *
  – 1st generation referral 50/50 *
- Mentor is responsible for new associate's contract validation.
- Any deviation of this agreement must be agreed upon by both the Mentor and the Mentee.

_____
Mentor   Date

_____
Mentee   Date

North Star Apprentice/Mentor Split Case Agreement

North Star Resource Group provides an apprenticeship program whereby a mentor is assigned to each apprentice. The purpose of the program is to assist the apprentice in achieving increased effectiveness over a period of six (6) months.

While the mentor provides coaching and direction, it is the sole responsibility of the apprentice to meet the expectations of North Star Resource Group by implementing the programs and procedures in a timely, efficient manner within the program parameters.

During the period of the mentoring program, commissions for products and services obtained by the client(s) will be split between the mentor and the apprentice as follows*:

Pre-Quick Start (Months 1-2)
Commission Split: 50% Mentor/50% Apprentice*
- Apprentice obtains name of referral/prospect.
- Apprentice books appointments.
- Apprentice observes mentor in facilitation of all appointment(s): Opener, Fact Finding/Present Plan, Closing*(1).

Quick Start (Months 3-4)
Commission Split: 50% Mentor/50% Apprentice*
- Apprentice obtains name of referral/prospect.
- Apprentice books appointments.
- Apprentice conducts Opener and facilitates Fact Finder/Present Plan on basic cases*(1).
- Apprentice observes mentor in all other facets.

Career Development Program (Months 5-6)
Commission Split: 50% Mentor/50% Apprentice*
- Apprentice obtains names of referral/prospect.
- Apprentice books appointments.
- Apprentice conducts Opener and Fact Finder/Present Plan on basic cases.
- Apprentice participates in case preparation on basic client cases with mentor.

- Apprentice conducts closing on basic client cases with mentor*(1).
- Apprentice observes mentor in all other facets.

Each apprentice will be evaluated at the end of the six (6) month period. At that time, additional options, based on that evaluation and the needs of the apprentice may be implemented with the apprentice.

My signature below indicates acceptance and understanding of the Apprentice/Mentor Split Case Agreement as outlined.

_____

Apprentice Signature   Date

*These splits are subject to change based on mentor's discretion – MDRT split should be honored when appropriate.
*(1) Apprentice can conduct meetings by self upon approval of Training Coordinator and Mentor after video boot camp.

North Star New Associate Apprenticeship Program

Pre-Quick Start
- From Business Marketing Plan, contact those listed to schedule Center of Influence (COI) meetings positioning your Mentor.
- Go on COI meetings with your Mentor.
- Gather introductions/referrals from each COI meeting to begin building your 100 qualified referrals/introductions.
- Schedule 1st meetings with those referred to you by your COI meetings.
- Attend with Mentor the Present Plan/Fact Finding meeting.
- Send daily email to Ed, Mentor and Tracie reporting your daily activity.
- Pass exams (Life, Accident & Health and Securities).

Compensation
- You are networking, building relationships and procuring introductions to get your practices off to a fast start.
- Once you have acquired 100 qualified introductions/referrals and receive a recommendation and approval by your Mentor, you will graduate to the next tier in the professional process: Quick Start.
- Quick Start compensation is $1,000.00 per month.

Recruiter Initials _____

Candidate Initials _____

Training Coordinator Initials _____

Quick Start
- Schedule 1st meetings with those referred to you.
- Move through the client meeting process with Mentor.
- Complete 25 Fact Finding/Present Plan meetings with Mentor.
- Identify 10 people in the planning process whom Mentor believes will purchase life insurance.
- Report weekly activity on e-scoreboard.
- Send daily email to Ed, Mentor and Tracie reporting your daily activity.

Compensation
- Fifty percent commission on all sales.*
- $1,000.00 available in each of the two Quick Start months.
- Now eligible to participate in Minnesota Life's full-time agent benefit plan.
- Once you have acquired 25 Fact Finder and/or 10 life insurance applications submitted and upon recommendation and approval by your Mentor, you will graduate to the next tier in the professional process: Career Development Program (CDP).
- CDP Compensation: Months 1-4 = $2,000.00.

*Based on Mentor's discretion

Career Development Program (CDP)
- Schedule a minimum of five 1st appointments per week.
- Continue to hold meetings with Mentor.
- Continue to report activity on e-scoreboard on a weekly basis.
- Maintain a minimum of 120 monthly activity points through e-scoreboard.
- For 1st CDP period, send daily activity email to Ed, Mentor and Tracie.
- Become a LEAP licensed practitioner.
- Attend group Sales Builder meetings.

Compensation
- Period 1
  – $2,000 available per month.
  – 50% commissions on sales.*
  – $2,000 bonus at the end of period 1 if commission and activity are sufficient.
- Period 2-9
  – Please see attached spreadsheet. (Not included in this appendix.)

*Based on Mentor's discretion

North Star
Quarterly Review Questionnaire

Name: _____
Review Date: _____
Start year: _____

What is your key year-end goal?

What is your critical number?

Are you ahead or behind?

By how much?

Do you want to adjust your goal or your activity?

What is your motivation to hit your goal?

What is your primary market?

What market would you ideally want to work in?

What is your Life Production goal this year?

Are you ahead or behind?

By how much?

How many Appointments on your Books (AOB) do you have?

What is your hourly rate?
How many hours per week are you with clients?

How many new clients did you acquire last quarter?

What will you do differently to increase income?

How many potential new clients are on your books?

What are your greatest challenges (in order)?
1.
2.
3.

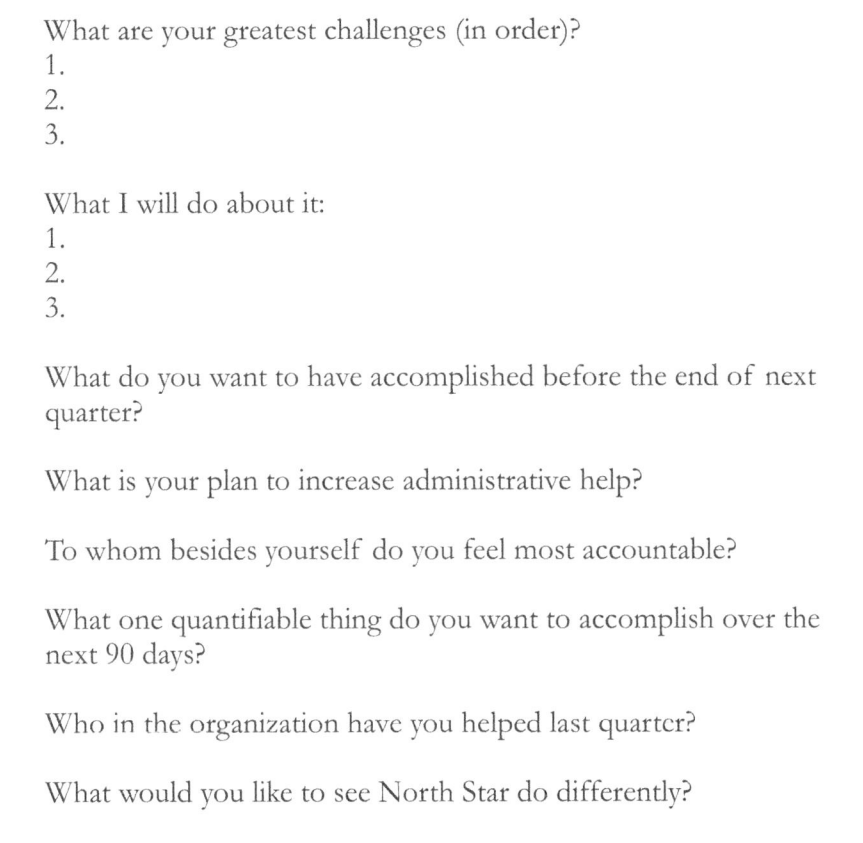

What I will do about it:
1.
2.
3.

What do you want to have accomplished before the end of next quarter?

What is your plan to increase administrative help?

To whom besides yourself do you feel most accountable?

What one quantifiable thing do you want to accomplish over the next 90 days?

Who in the organization have you helped last quarter?

What would you like to see North Star do differently?

What would you like to see Securian do differently?

North Star Value Proposition

The Marketing Initiatives we offer include:

- Firm Branded Financial Planning newsletter
- Firm Branded Investment/Money Management newsletter
- High-Quality, Firm-Branded (and advisor-tailored) brochure
- High-Quality, Firm-Branded (and advisor-tailored) Web site
- Firm-Branded, published book on financial planning (Real-Life Financial Planning)
- Marketing Assistant program
- Established client resource center for additional clients/appointments

In addition, other benefits that are accessible include:

- Health insurance coverage for advisor, spouse and family
- Group and supplemental disability insurance
- Group life insurance coverage (both basic and supplemental)
- 401(k) plan with matching contribution
- Support for marketing, assistant, technology
- National Sales Conventions (based on production) —Recent meeting locations have been Palm Desert, CA, and Marco Island, FL.
- International Leaders Conference (based on production) — Recent meeting locations have been Edinburgh, Scotland, and Sydney, Australia.
- Annual meeting for top investment advisors (Circle of Excellence) — Recent meeting locations have New York City, Vancouver, British Columbia and Washington, D.C.
- Rewards trips and prizes — Every-other-year annual event to lodge in Northern Wisconsin and additional night's stay in the convention city.
- In-house training meetings on various investment, insurance and financial planning topics
- In-house Advanced Case Training classes
- In-house Long Term Care Department
- In-house Employee Benefits Department
- In-house Insurance Brokerage Department

- Access to subsidized advanced training meetings on various investment, insurance and financial planning topics
- In-house continuing education (CE) opportunities
- Fully paid Million Dollar Round Table (MDRT) annual dues
- Subsidized MDRT meeting registration fees
- Firm Alignment and Reward (FAR) Plan (LFF stock plan for advisors)
- TIA (Transition Incentive Assistance Plan (succession planning for seasoned advisors to transition their practice)
- Very competitive payouts
- Leads generated through in-house "orphan program" and "call center"
- Payroll processing for administrative/marketing assistants
- Commitment to New Organization's growth to provide additional revenue opportunities through joint work
- Commitment to New Organization growth to enable seasoned advisors to reassign clients/households who do not fit their business model
- North Star Charitable Giving Foundation

Our value proposition at North Star Resource Group is that we will create an environment dedicated to the advancement of your career, giving you the greatest opportunity for success available in the financial services industry. We have built this environment over the past 40 years and continue to be considered a leader in this industry.

Resources we will provide you to maximize your productivity and profitability include:

- In-house estate planning/business planning/elder care attorney
- In-house investment specialists
- In-house financial planning specialists
- In-house certified public accountant/tax specialist
- In-house Long Term Care Insurance Department
- In-house new business (underwriting) processing team
- In-house compliance support and oversight
- In-house recruiters to grow our manpower development
- In-house technology specialists

- Affiliated with property & casualty insurance provider (both commercial and personal lines)
- Affiliated with third-party administration (TPA) for qualified plans
- Unlimited access to top-quality investment management firms

In addition to these resources, we offer numerous technology and marketing initiatives, as well as a number of additional benefits.

Technology and software sponsored or supported by our firm include:

- Morningstar Fund Analytics
- Morningstar Advisor Workstation
- Financial Profiles
- Naviplan
- Financial Forecaster
- Client Connect (Client Management System)
- Albridge (Client reporting system)
- Back-Room Technician
- Harmony Illustration System
- Bisys Illustration Platform

APPENDIX   251

North Star/Moss-Adams Findings...

- Presented by David Vasos, Executive VP
  February 2007

Approximately six months ago Philip Palaveev of Moss Adams presented some summary findings regarding how Independent Broker Dealer firms compared to Affiliated Firms in terms of "Gross" and "Net" payouts. This information was generic in nature and lacked any specific comparison to North Star or any particular Independent Broker-Dealer (IBD). At that meeting, we made a public commitment to charge Philip and Moss Adams with the task of comparing North Star's specific compensation and expense arrangements with a hand picked list of 9 IBD's. Without knowing the ultimate outcome, we indicated that if gaps were identified we would take appropriate action to close those gaps and ensure that North Star's value proposition remained fair and competitive relative to the competition. I'm proud to say that we took a first step on this commitment by recently instituting a retroactive Incentive GDC Bonus for Housed Associates producing above the top of the Grid in securities GDC.

After six months of data compilation, analysis and evaluation I am also pleased to share with you a summary of the major conclusions of this study.

Methodology:

Moss-Adams utilized specific North Star compensation schedules for both internal and detached associates based on 4 different production profiles. These profiles covered a range of production mixes from heavy insurance to high growth, balanced and heavy securities emphasis. These four specific profiles were then compared to the actual compensation available from 9 selected IBD's based on total GDC from insurance and securities. Moss-Adams relied upon its proprietary survey of over 1000 advisors in comparing common expenses for both North Star and the Independent BD's (this survey is the oldest and most authoritative source of practice level data covering advisors' financial and operating performance). Wherever possible, actual North Star expense levels were used and all other expenses were applied uniformly to both North Star and the Independent BD's using the expense levels indicated by the survey results for specific levels of production. This methodology provided a common platform upon which to measure the top line and bottom line financial results for both North Star and the Independent BD's.

Summary Conclusion:

Based on the analysis conducted, Moss-Adams found that across all four profiles, "North Star compensation is competitive with the rest of the industry." Specifically, when differences in production profiles are considered: "North Star compensation is the highest of all models considered for Chairman's Club Advisors (high insurance producers). Further, North Star compensation is the highest for Growth Advisors (high growth in both insurance and securities) and North Star compensation is competitive for Blend (50/50 mix) and Securities focused advisors."

Growth Advisor Example: Getting to the Bottom Line:

Bottom Line = Nominal Payout
+ Additional Cash Compensation (Production Bonus, Securian "cash" benefits at cost - FICA Match, 401k match, subsidized Health Insurance...)
+ Non cash Compensation (Recognition, Deferred Compensation etc. at cost) less all "common" expenses expressed as a percentage of GDC.

The "Growth Advisor" charts to the left clearly show the expense advantage of the Housed advisor who is able to take advantage of North Star's size and scale

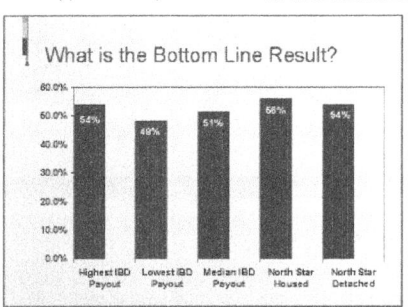

What is the Bottom Line Result?

Highest IBD Payout	54%
Lowest IBD Payout	49%
Median IBD Payout	51%
North Star Housed	56%
North Star Detached	54%

MOSS-ADAMS LLP

Overall Results

- North Star Housed is 104.5% of the highest independent broker-dealer payout
- North Star Detached is at 102.1% of the highest broker-dealer payout
- North Star Housed advisors pay 17.1% of total compensation towards expenses, compared to an average of 43.1% paid by independent broker-dealer affiliated advisors

MOSS-ADAMS LLP

Overall Results

	Typical Broker-Dealer	North Star Housed	North Star Detached
Top line Compensation	271,200	202,601	270,481
Total Expenses	115,340	34,718	106,243
Bottom-line compensation	153,470	167,883	164,038

MOSS-ADAMS

Overall Results – Chairman's Club

- North Star Housed achieves 104% of the highest independent broker-dealer payout at $361,999 net income
- North Star Detached is competitive with independent broker-dealers at 99% ($348,103) of the highest broker dealer payout
- North Star Housed advisors pay 12.6% of total compensation towards expenses, compared to an average of 38.8% paid by independent broker-dealer affiliated advisors

MOSS-ADAMS

Overall Results – Blend Advisor

- North Star Housed achieves 92.5% of the highest independent broker-dealer payout at $163,117 net income – a level we consider competitive
- North Star Detached is competitive with independent broker dealers at 95.9% ($187,008) of the highest broker-dealer payout
- North Star Housed advisors pay 15.5% of total compensation towards expenses, compared to an average of 38.0% paid by independent broker-dealer affiliated advisors

MOSS-ADAMS

Overall Results – Securities Advisor

- North Star Housed is competitive at 94.3% of the highest independent broker dealer payout
- North Star Detached is competitive at 93.2% of the highest independent broker-dealer payout
- North Star Housed advisors pay 17.1% of total compensation towards expenses, compared to an average of 41.80% paid by independent broker-dealer affiliated advisors

MOSS-ADAMS

In leveraging the resources provided to housed advisors which would have to be reproduced at an additional cost in the detached and independent BD models.

Specific Conclusions: What makes North Star Competitive?

- The North Star Housed Model has significant expense advantages. This provides producers within each profile the "ability to leverage the support structure of the housed model and not incur the staffing costs for additional administrative help (reception, IT, general administration, compliance, internal accounting." The Housed model also affords lower equipment and IT related expenses as well as lower overall infrastructure expenses (phone, internet, network, etc.).

- The Housed Model affords significant additional cash benefits either as expense reimbursements or added direct compensation benefits as a result of the Internal Support Credits earned, especially at higher levels of production." The value of North Star Credits can represent as much as 10% to 13% of total bottom line results."

- Strong Bonus programs and Employee Benefit and Recognition programs add value to all associates – housed and detached." These benefits can add as much as 5% to total bottom line results."

- "The North Star model" compares well at the bottom line to Independent broker dealer advisors. In addition, North Star's flexible affiliation model "allows advisors with diverse practice models to receive industry standard compensation" regardless of being housed or detached.

Perhaps more significantly, the quantitative analysis above includes no "value" for what we believe to be one of North Star's principal strengths – the cultural fit, opportunity for practice growth and significant practice support available to all advisors in the North Star model.

There is much more in this report than can be summarized in one article but the bottom line should be clear — regardless of your affiliation (housed or detached) and regardless of your practice profile you have a fair and competitive compensation arrangement relative to the industry. I would welcome anyone with any questions to contact me for more information. In addition, we will be keeping this information current by way of periodic updates and will look for future opportunities to have Moss-Adams share their results directly with you.

APPENDIX

Conclusions
(Excerpts from Moss Adams presentation)

MOSS-ADAMS LLP

The Conclusion

- North Star compensation is competitive with the rest of the industry
- When differences in production profiles are considered:
  - North Star compensation is the highest of all models considered* for Chairman's Club Advisors
  - North Star compensation is the highest for growth advisors
  - North Star compensation is competitive for blend and securities focused advisors

* The models considered were: Growth Advisor, Blend Advisor, Mature Securities and Chairman's Club Advisor. Characteristics of each model were determined and provided by North Star to Moss Adams LLP

MOSS-ADAMS LLP

Conclusions

- **The expense advantage of the North Star housed model:**
  - Ability to leverage the support structure of housed model and not have to incur the staffing cost for additional administrative help
    - Reception, IT, general administration, compliance, internal accounting
  - Lower equipment and IT related expenses
  - Lower infrastructure expenses – phone, internet, etc.
- **Value of North Star credits in the housed model**
  - Represent 10% to 13% of the total bottom-line
- **Value of North Star\Securian benefits and recognition to all associates**
  - ~5% of bottom-line results

MOSS-ADAMS LLP

Conclusions

- **Potential gaps under consideration:**
  - The support provided through the credits is not sufficient and advisors need to pay for additional help:
    - Structure of the practice and workflow
    - Are these the optimal clients?
    - Is the business mix streamlined – i.e. too many lines of business or too much customization?
  - Service needs that do not fit the support infrastructure
  - What if an advisor does not value the benefits – health, recognition, etc.
  - Product mix and tenure have some impact on credits

MOSS-ADAMS LLP

Overall Conclusions

- The North Star model compares well at the bottom line to independent broker-dealer advisors
- The model allows advisors with diverse practice models to receive industry standard compensation

- Economic analysis is only one consideration
  - Cultural fit
  - Opportunity for practice growth
  - Significant practice support

MOSS-ADAMS LLP